Apple Pencil Pro User Manual

How to Set Up, Draw, Write, and Customize Using Your iPad (2024 Edition)

Nico Grey

Table of Contents

INTRODUCTION 1

CHAPTER ONE: 3

FEATURES OF THE APPLE PENCIL PRO 3

SQUEEZE TO ACCESS TOOLS 4

2. HAPTIC FEEDBACK 6

3. BARREL ROLLS 8

4. FIND MY SUPPORT 9

5. APPLE PENCIL HOVER 10

6. DOUBLE TAP 12

7. USB-C 14

THREE APPLE PENCIL PRO FEATURES THAT MIGHT CHANGE
DIGITAL ARTISTS' WORKFLOWS 15

Barrel Roll 15

Haptic Engine 16

Find my support 17

CHAPTER TWO: 18

GET STARTED WITH YOUR APPLE PENCIL PRO 18

HOW TO PAIR AND CHARGE APPLE PENCIL PRO WITH IPAD 19

WAYS TO CHECK THE BATTERY LEVEL OF APPLE PENCIL 24

HOW TO CHECK THE APPLE PENCIL BATTERY PERCENTAGE WITH
SETTINGS 27

ENTER TEXT WITH SCRIBBLE ON THE IPAD 28

HOW TO USE APPLE PENCIL TO ENTER TEXT IN ANY TEXT FIELD
.... 30

HOW TO USE APPLE PENCIL TO ENTER TEXT IN NOTES AND
FREEFORM.. 33

ENABLING SCRIBBLE.. 33

ENTERING AND EDITING TEXT IN NOTES 34

HOW TO CHOOSE TEXT AND CHANGE IT WITH APPLE PENCIL. 36

HOW TO STOP CONVERTING YOUR HANDWRITING TO TEXT... 40

HOW TO DRAW WITH APPLE PENCIL ON IPAD 44

HOW TO DRAW ON THE IPAD: PAIR YOUR APPLE PENCIL......... 45

HOW TO APPLY SHADING AND DARKER LINES 55

HOW TO DOUBLE-TAP TO SWITCH TOOLS 59

HOW TO SQUEEZE APPLE PENCIL PRO TO PERFORM ACTION.. 64

HOW TO TURN HAPTIC FEEDBACK FOR APPLE PENCIL PRO OFF
OR ON.. 66

HOVER TO PREVIEW TOOLS AND CONTROLS 68

HOW TO TAKE AND MARK UP A SCREENSHOT WITH APPLE
PENCIL ON IPAD... 71

CHAPTER THREE: 75

CREATE QUICK NOTES ANYWHERE ON THE IPAD......... 75

HOW TO MAKE A QUICK NOTE 79

HOW TO REOPEN OR LINK BACK TO A QUICK NOTE 80

WHERE TO FIND ALL YOUR QUICK NOTES 81

HOW TO VIEW AND ORGANIZE QUICK NOTES 81

HOW TO CHANGE OR DISABLE THE CORNER GESTURE FOR QUICK NOTES. 83

CHAPTER FOUR: 86

DO MORE WITH THE APPLE PENCIL PRO 86

WRITE A QUICK NOTE 86

GATHER IDEAS IN FREEFORM.................................... 88

CONVERT HANDWRITING INTO TYPED TEXT 91

MARK UP A SCREENSHOT 93

CHAPTER FIVE: 97

HOW TO ADD AND EDIT DRAWINGS ON YOUR IPAD USING THE APPLE PENCIL PRO 97

HOW TO ADD A DRAWING.. 97

HOW TO EDIT DRAWINGS 102

HOW TO SEPARATE A DRAWING INTO PARTS 109

HOW TO ANIMATE A DRAWING............................... 114

CHANGE OBJECT TRANSPARENCY IN PAGES ON THE IPAD 121

CHAPTER SIX:.. 123

HOW TO ADD A REFLECTION OR SHADOW IN PAGES ON IPAD. 123

HOW TO ADD REFLECTION...................................... 123

HOW TO ADD SHADOW 125

WAYS TO USE LAYER, GROUP, AND LOCK OBJECTS IN PAGES ON IPAD 128

HOW TO USE LAYER OBJECT 131

HOW TO GROUP OR UNGROUP OBJECTS 132

HOW TO LOCK OR UNLOCK OBJECT 134

HOW TO POSITION ITEMS 137

HOW TO MOVE, ROTATE, OR RESIZE AN ITEM 139

CHAPTER SEVEN: 142

HOW TO PLACE OBJECTS WITH TEXT ON PAGES ON IPAD 142

HOW TO ANCHOR AN OBJECT TO THE PAGE OR TEXT 145

HOW TO WRAP TEXT AROUND AN OBJECT 147

HOW TO SHOW OR HIDE THE RULER ON PAGES ON IPAD 149

CHAPTER EIGHT: 150

HOW TO DRAW OR HANDWRITE ON A FREEFORM BOARD ON
IPAD 150

WAYS TO ADD SHAPES, LINES, ARROWS, AND DIAGRAMS TO A
FREEFORM BOARD ON IPAD 153

HOW TO ADD AND FORMAT SHAPES, LINES, AND ARROWS .. 156

HOW TO SPLIT OR COMBINE SHAPE 158

HOW TO CHANGE SIZE, WIDTH, OR LENGTH 161

CHAPTER NINE: 164

HOW TO USE MARKUP TO ADD TEXT, SHAPES, SIGNATURES,
AND MORE TO DOCUMENTS ON IPAD 164

HOW TO ADD TEXT 164

HOW TO ADD AND EDIT TYPED TEXT 167

HOW TO ADD A SHAPE 170

HOW TO DRAW A SHAPE 176

HOW TO ADD YOUR SIGNATURE............................. 179

HOW TO ADD OR DELETE SIGNATURES AND HOW TO ADD A STICKER WITH MARKUP 183

HOW TO ADD CUSTOM IMAGE DESCRIPTIONS 187

HOW TO ENTER TEXT WITH SCRIBBLE ON IPAD...................... 190

HOW TO USE APPLE PENCIL TO ENTER TEXT IN NOTES AND FREEFORM.. 194

HOW TO CHOOSE TEXT AND CHANGE IT WITH APPLE PENCIL197

HOW TO STOP CONVERTING YOUR HANDWRITING TO TEXT. 200

HOW TO TAKE AND MARK UP A SCREENSHOT WITH APPLE PENCIL ON IPAD.. 201

CHAPTER TEN: 205

TIPS AND TRICKS 205

HOW TO OPEN NOTIFICATION CENTER................................ 206

HOW TO GO TO THE HOME SCREEN 209

HOW TO CREATE QUICK NOTES EVEN WHEN THE IPAD IS LOCKED... 210

HOW TO BRING UP A SKETCH PAD WINDOW FROM ANYWHERE 213

HOW TO GRAB A SCREENSHOT USING YOUR APPLE PENCIL (OR FINGER) 215

HOW TO TURN OFF LEFT AND RIGHT CORNER SWIPES TO PREVENT UNNECESSARY ACTIONS.................................. 217

HOW TO USE SCRIBBLE IN TEXT FIELDS 219

HOW TO WRITE WITH APPLE PENCIL AND CONVERT INTO TYPED TEXT.. 220

HOW TO COPY WHAT YOU'VE ALREADY WRITTEN WITH APPLE PENCIL AS NORMAL TYPED TEXT 223

HOW TO TAKE RELEVANT ACTION ON WRITTEN TEXT 225

SIGN PDFS AND DOCUMENTS... 230

HOW TO DRAW PERFECT SHAPES 233

HOW TO TILT YOUR APPLE PENCIL TIP 235

HOW TO USE PRESSURE SENSITIVITY...................................... 238

HOW TO DRAW ON A PIECE OF ACTUAL PAPER WITH YOUR APPLE PENCIL AND HAVE IT APPEAR ON YOUR IPAD.............. 243

HOW TO DRAW IN EMAILS... 247

HOW TO USE TWO FINGERS TO SCROLL WHEN DRAWING WITH APPLE PENCIL 251

HOW TO TURN HOVER OFF OR ON 254

INTRODUCTION

In a world where touchscreens have become the canvas for our ideas, Apple has quietly pushed the boundaries once more. The Apple Pencil Pro isn't just another stylus; it's a portal to a new dimension of creativity, precision, and productivity. Beneath its sleek aluminium body lies a suite of features so thoughtfully engineered that, until now, most users have only scratched the surface of what it can truly do.

This book is your definitive guide to mastering the Apple Pencil Pro from the moment you unbox it. We begin by walking through an effortless setup and pairing with no cables, no fumbling, just a simple magnetic tap that brings your stylus to life. From there, you'll learn how to keep your Pencil charged and ready, and how to monitor its battery at a glance, so that inspiration never has to wait for a power cycle.

Next, we'll delve into the art of interaction: the subtle hover effects that preview your touch, the satisfying precision haptics that let you feel every snap-to-centre and swipe, and the twin gestures, squeeze and double-tap, that put tool switching, undo/redo, and colour palettes literally at your fingertips. You'll discover how tilt, barrel-roll, and pressure sensitivity combine to deliver natural pencil-and-brush emulation, transforming your iPad into a virtuosic sketchpad or a finely tuned note-taking machine.

Beyond the basics, we'll explore advanced workflows and hidden gems: converting rough shapes into perfect geometry, turning handwritten notes into editable text, signing contracts in seconds, and even harnessing the Find My network so you never lose track of your stylus again. Finally, I'll introduce you to the best apps like Procreate, Astro Pad Studio, Freeform, GoodNotes , and more that have been reimagined around the Pro's unique capabilities, ensuring that whatever your passion, illustration, design, teaching, or brainstorming. You have the perfect toolkit at hand.

Whether you're a digital artist seeking pixel-perfect control or a professional who treats your iPad as your primary workstation, this book will unlock the latent power of the Apple Pencil Pro. Turn the page, and let's embark on a journey to reshape what's possible when pen meets pixel.

CHAPTER ONE:

FEATURES OF THE APPLE PENCIL PRO

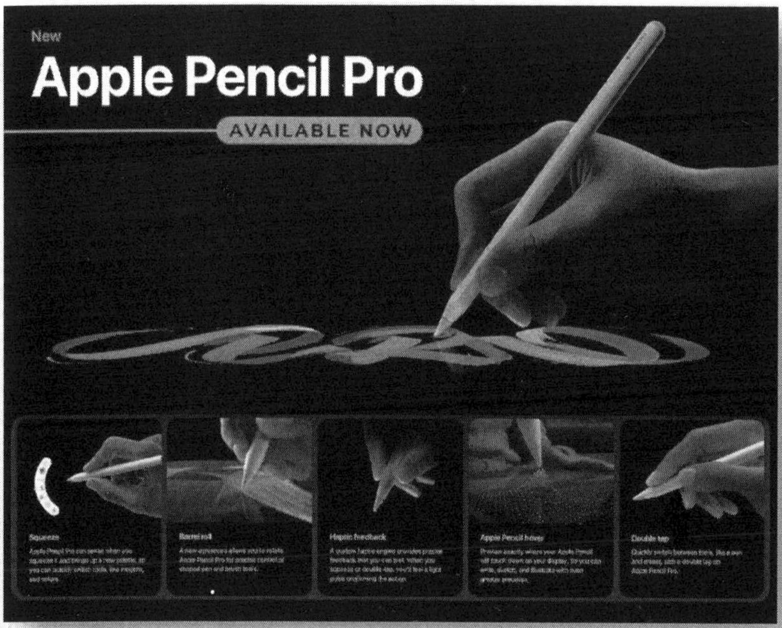

SQUEEZE TO ACCESS TOOLS

A new sensor in the Apple Pencil Pro enables users to squeeze the accessory to

Display a tool palette, allowing quick access to switch tools, adjust line weights, and

change colours.

In addition, a newly integrated gyroscope lets users rotate the Apple Pencil Pro for more

precise control when using shaped pen and brush tools.

With the addition of a new haptic engine, the Apple Pencil Pro delivers a light tap as

feedback when users perform actions such as squeezing, double-tapping, or snapping to a

Smart Shape.

What it does:

The squeeze gesture allows the Apple Pencil Pro to detect pressure applied to the sides of

the device. When squeezed, a palette appears, enabling users to switch tools, line weights,

and colours. Developers can also customize app behaviour for the squeeze gesture,

allowing it to trigger unique controls within each app.

1. Open the Settings app.

2. Select Apple Pencil.

3. Tap Squeeze.

4. Choose one of the following functions:

· Show Tool Palette

· Switch Between Current Tool and Eraser

· Switch Between Current Tool and Last Used

· Show Colour Palette

· Show Ink Attributes

·Shortcut

· Off

Customization: In Settings → Apple Pencil, you can assign the squeeze gesture to

functions like "Switch to Eraser," "Undo/Redo," "Show Colour Palette," or app-specific

shortcuts in apps like Procreate

By default, the Squeeze gesture opens the tool palette in the app you're currently using

(such as Apple Notes or Freeform). However, you can customize what the Squeeze

gesture does; you can even assign it to trigger a shortcut.

2. HAPTIC FEEDBACK

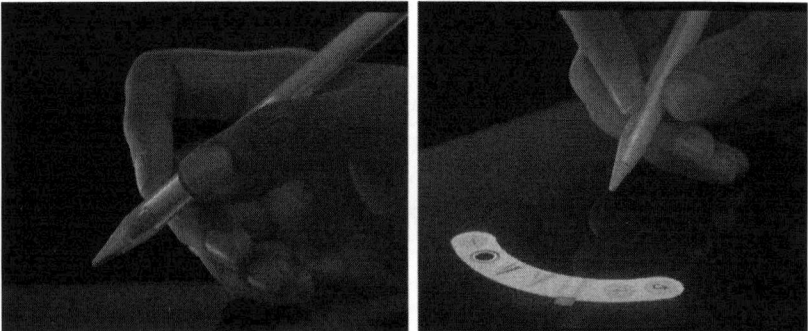

The Apple Pencil Pro incorporates a **custom haptic engine**, similar to the Taptic Engine in other Apple devices that delivers **precise, low-latency tactile pulses** whenever users perform gestures like **squeeze** or **double-tap**, providing immediate confirmation of actions and enhancing immersion during creative workflows. This haptic system is driven by a micro-vibration actuator controlled by onboard circuitry—among them a Cirrus Logic CS35L91 amplifier—enabling finely tuned feedback patterns that can simulate brush rotation, tool switching, and even textured paper sensations Users can adjust the **strength** and **sensitivity** of these feedback pulses in iPadOS settings, and developers can leverage Apple's APIs to create **custom haptic interactions** in apps like Procreate, further expanding the expressive potential of the stylus

3. BARREL ROLLS

The Apple Pencil Pro features a built-in gyroscope that detects how the barrel is rotated,

allowing it to adjust the direction and angle of certain tools on screen. This enables users

to have greater precision and control, especially when using shaped pens or brushes. It

simulates the natural movement of a traditional pen or paintbrush, responding to how you tilt and turn the pencil while sketching or drawing. It enables users to spin the Pencil to

rotate the virtual brush. In the real world, if you're holding a paintbrush and need to make a

different stroke, you can just rotate it in your hand. Barrel roll simulates this effect

4. FIND MY SUPPORT

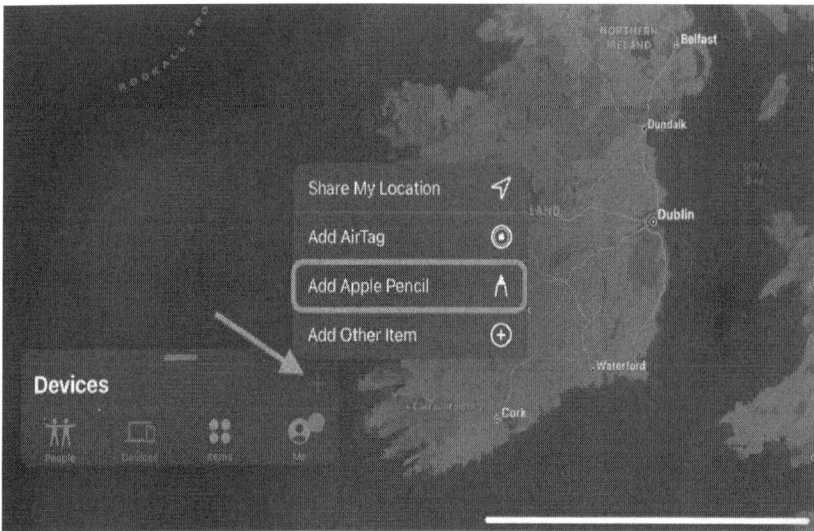

The Apple Pencil Pro is compatible with the Find My feature, allowing it to be tracked just

like your iPad or other Apple devices within the Find My app. However, unlike certain Apple products that include an Ultra Wideband (UWB) chip, the Apple Pencil Pro relies on

Bluetooth to help locate it through the app.

During the initial setup, you should see an option to add Apple Pencil Pro to Find My. If it

doesn't appear after pairing, you can manually add it by following these steps:

1. Open the Find My app.

2. Tap the plus (+) icon.

3. Select Add Apple Pencil.

5. APPLE PENCIL HOVER

The Apple Pencil Pro (2024) includes an advanced hover feature that lets you preview your mark before you touch the iPad screen. It works by detecting the pencil's tip up to mm above the display, using signals processed by the iPad's chip (like the M4 or M2).

When you hover, the screen shows a visual indicator or brush outline under the tip, allowing

for precise strokes, colour drops, and tool previews in creative apps like Procreate, Apple

Notes, and more. You can see brush size, colour effects, and even UI elements respond to

your Pencil's movement before drawing or tapping. This feature improves:

· Accuracy (you see exactly where the stroke will land),

· Workflow (no more trial-and-error),

· And interaction (hovering highlights icons, previews colours, and aligns strokes precisely).

Compared to older Apple Pencils, this version also brings wider compatibility (across iPad

Pro, Air, and Mini) and works seamlessly without setup. For artists and designers, it feels like having a real-time digital cursor, making drawing and editing faster and more intuitive.

6. DOUBLE TAP

The Double-Tap function, first introduced with the Apple Pencil 2, is also available on the

Apple Pencil Pro. It enables users to carry out actions like opening the colour palette or

switching back to the previously used tool.

This feature also allows for touch-free selection; you can simply hover the Apple Pencil over an item and double-tap its side to select it.

To customize what the Double-Tap does, follow these steps:

1. Open the Settings app.

2. Tap Apple Pencil.

3. Select Double-Tap.

4. Choose one of the following options:

- Switch Between Current Tool and Eraser
- Switch Between Current Tool and Last Used
- Show Colour Palette
- Show Ink Attributes
- Off

7. USB-C

Charging and connectivity have been made more convenient thanks to a new magnetic

interface. The Apple Pencil Pro can magnetically attach to the side of supported iPads,

allowing for effortless charging. There is also a USB-C option available as an alternative charging method. Pairing is simple and user-friendly, with no complicated setup required, and the connection

remains stable and secure.

THREE APPLE PENCIL PRO FEATURES THAT MIGHT CHANGE DIGITAL ARTISTS' WORKFLOWS

Barrel Roll

Think of a real paintbrush or pencil: artists often twist it to change the stroke angle. The Pencil Pro's **Barrel Roll** works the same way digitally. When you spin the pencil in your hand, the app rotates or changes the on-screen brush. For example, twisting it might tilt a flat brush or adjust a stroke's direction without you touching any menus. In practice, this means you can shade, sketch, or switch brush styles on the fly by simply rolling the pencil, making drawing feel more natural and fluid. Every small wrist motion shows up in your artwork, so you keep drawing without breaks to adjust tools.

Haptic Engine

The Pencil Pro has a tiny built-in motor that gives gentle feedback – a soft buzz or tap you can feel. This **Haptic Engine** comes alive when you do things like squeeze the pencil, hover over an item, or snap a drawing element into place. For artists, it adds a little physical "nudge" to the digital experience. For instance, when a line ends or a shape aligns perfectly, the pencil might vibrate briefly so you know you've hit your mark. This subtle tap makes the tool feel more real and helps you trust what you're doing on screen. You get a sense of touch to go with the visual, giving extra confidence when making precise strokes or switching tools.

Find my support

Losing a Favorite pen or pencil is frustrating, so Apple added **Find My** support to Pencil Pro. Now you can use the Find My app on your iPad or iPhone to see where your pencil was last used or make it nearby. If you accidentally leave it on a shelf or it slips under a couch cushion, the app will guide you to it. This feature is like a safety net for your workflow: instead of pausing to search or buying a new stylus, you quickly locate the missing pencil and get back to creating.

CHAPTER TWO:

GET STARTED WITH YOUR APPLE PENCIL PRO

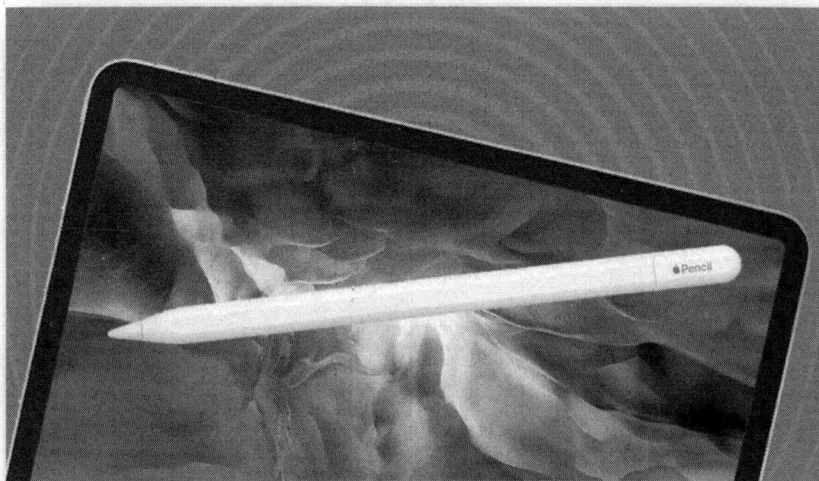

If you've recently purchased an iPad to support your creative or professional work, learning

how to connect and use an Apple Pencil is an important first step. Setting it up quickly

allows you to begin writing, sketching, or drawing without spending too much time

navigating the settings.

Once the Apple Pencil is connected to your iPad, you can take advantage of its many features, including note-taking, illustration, and using a wide range of compatible apps.

Whether they come pre-installed or are downloaded from the App Store.

Because there are different versions of the Apple Pencil and a variety of iPad models, it's

completely normal to feel unsure about how to connect the two. Many users have faced the

same situation, and this guide is here to help you get everything working smoothly.

HOW TO PAIR AND CHARGE APPLE PENCIL PRO WITH IPAD

Quick steps to connect your Apple Pencil to an iPad

There are four different Apple Pencil models. Two of them are currently supported with

updates: the Apple Pencil Pro and the Apple Pencil with USB-C. The other two are older versions, which include the original Apple Pencil and the Apple Pencil 2.

To use any of these styluses with your iPad, Bluetooth must be turned on. Below is how to

pair each model with your device:

• For the original Apple Pencil, remove the end cap and insert it into your iPad's Lightning

port.

• To connect the Apple Pencil 2, place it on the magnetic connector on the side of your

iPad. It will pair automatically.

• For the Apple Pencil with USB-C, remove the end cap and plug it into the USB-C port

on your iPad.

• The Apple Pencil Pro pairs in the same way as the second-generation version. Simply attach it to the magnetic connector on the iPad, and it will connect automatically.

Step-by-step guide for how to connect your Apple Pencil to an iPad

Let's take a closer look at the methods mentioned earlier. To begin, I'll guide you through how to enable Bluetooth on your iPad. After that, I'll explain the steps required to pair each type of Apple Pencil

Turning on your iPad's Bluetooth

Before you can use an Apple Pencil, you need to make sure that Bluetooth is enabled on your iPad. In most cases, Bluetooth may already be turned on, especially if you use other wireless accessories. However, if it's not, or if you just want to check, here's how to do it. Start by swiping down from the top-right corner of any screen on your iPad. This opens the quick settings menu. Look for the Bluetooth button, which is typically marked by the Bluetooth symbol. In some versions of iPadOS, the icon will appear right away. In others, it may be located inside an additional menu. Tapping that area will reveal more options, including Bluetooth.

If the Bluetooth icon, which looks like a stylized letter "B" made of straight lines, appears blue, then Bluetooth is already turned on. If the icon is Gray, it means Bluetooth is off. To enable it, tap directly on the icon. Avoid tapping the larger area labelled "Bluetooth, as this will open the list of connected devices rather than toggling the Bluetooth setting itself.

Pairing second-gen & USB-C Apple Pencil

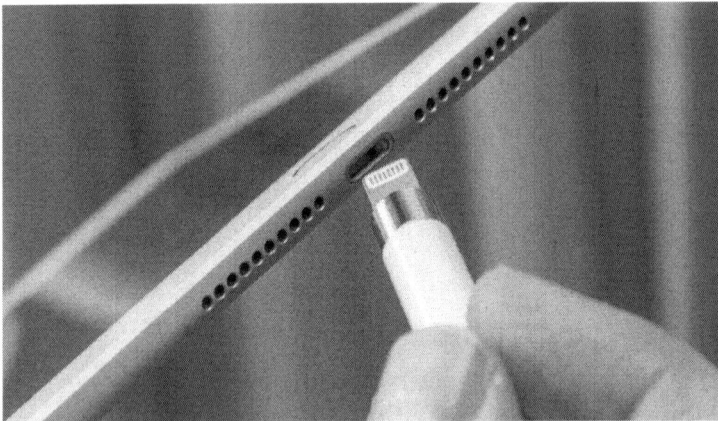

If your Apple Pencil does not have a visible connector, it is either the second-generation model or the Apple Pencil Pro. Both of these styluses connect to the iPad using the same method. To pair them, simply place the Apple Pencil against the magnetic area on the side of

your iPad. This magnetic strip is usually located along one of the longer edges of the device, often opposite the keyboard connectors. An easy way to locate it is to press the stylus gently against the edge of your iPad. If it clicks into place and holds securely, you've found the right spot. After the Apple Pencil attaches magnetically, it will pair with your iPad automatically. This same position also serves as the charging point for the stylus.

Pairing the second-gen and Pro Apple Pencil

If your Apple Pencil doesn't have a connector, then it's either the second-gen or Pro version of the Apple Pencil. Both connect in the same way.

To connect these Apple Pencils to an iPad, simply **attach them to the magnetic strip on your iPad**. This can be found along one of the length edges of the tablet, generally on the opposite side of the keyboard connectors. The easy way to find it is simply to put your Apple Pencil against the iPad and see if the magnets keep it secured!

Once you've attached your Apple Pencil to the iPad physically, it'll automatically pair so you can use your stylus. And this is also how you charge up your stylus.

WAYS TO CHECK THE BATTERY LEVEL OF APPLE PENCIL

How to check an Apple Pencil's charge with the battery widget

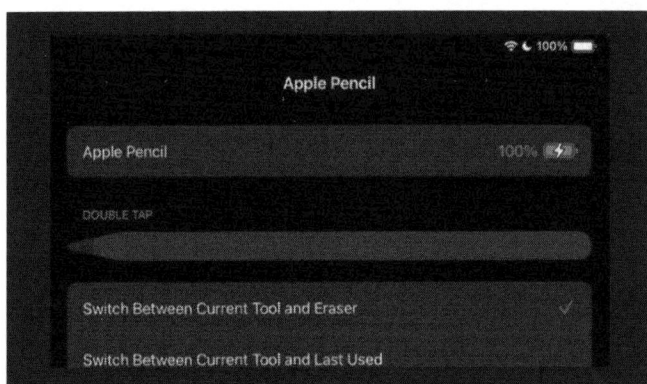

A convenient way to check how much battery your Apple Pencil has left is by using the battery widget that comes built into your iPad. If you haven't tried using widgets before, this one is a good starting point. It displays your iPad's battery percentage, along with the charge levels of other Apple devices connected to it, including the Apple Watch, AirPods, and the Apple Pencil. To add the battery widget to your home screen, begin by pressing and holding a blank space on the screen. Once the layout enters edit mode, tap the plus icon at the top left corner. From the widget options, scroll until you locate the section labelled "Batteries." This widget comes in three sizes: small, medium, and large. To make sure the Apple Pencil appears, select either the medium or large size, as the small one may not show all connected devices. No matter which version of the Apple Pencil you are using, whether it's the first generation, the second generation, or the USB-C model, you should be able to see its battery status as long as it is connected to your iPad and within range. If the stylus is paired but still does not appear in the widget, it might be completely out of charge.

How to check an Apple Pencil's battery percentage with an iPad

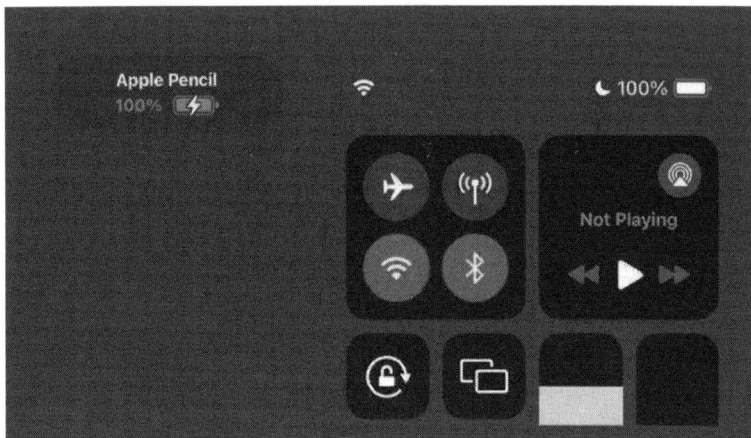

One of the simplest ways to check the battery level of your Apple Pencil is by connecting it. Directly to your iPad. Although the Apple Pencil with USB-C can attach magnetically, it Does not support wireless charging. Because of this limitation, this method only works with The second-generation Apple Pencil. If you are using the Apple Pencil 2, just place it on the magnetic strip along the side of Your iPad. When it connects, a notification will appear at the top of the screen, showing the The current battery percentage of the stylus. Since this attachment point is also how the Apple Pencil charges; this method provides both battery status and charging at the same time Time. In case the battery level pop-up does not appear immediately, try removing the Apple. Pencil and attaching it again. If there is still no response, the stylus might be completely. Drained. Leave it connected for a short time; it will begin to charge within a few seconds. And should automatically reconnect to the iPad once it has enough power.

HOW TO CHECK THE APPLE PENCIL BATTERY PERCENTAGE WITH SETTINGS

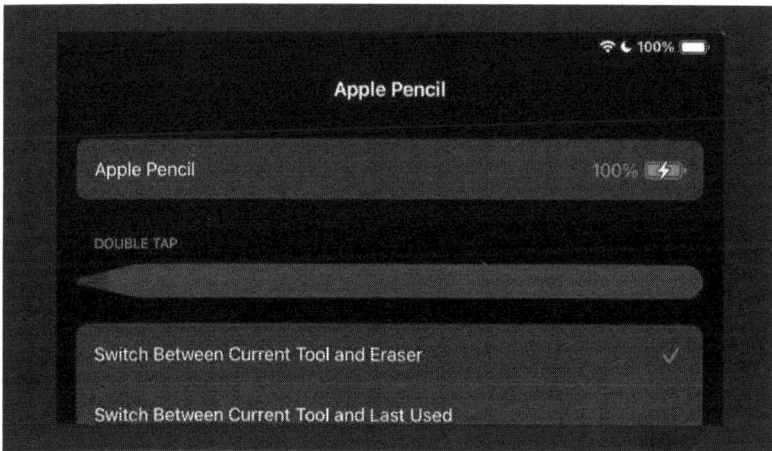

Another option for checking your Apple Pencil's battery level is through the Settings app on your iPad.

This method works with the original Apple Pencil, the second-generation model, and the newer USB-C version. As long as your Apple Pencil is paired with your iPad, you can view its battery status easily. To begin, open the Settings app and navigate to the Bluetooth section. Under the "My Devices" list, you should see your Apple Pencil listed. Tap the information icon (the letter "i") next to its name, and you will be taken to a screen where the current battery percentage is displayed. There is also a second method within the same app. Open the Settings app again and scroll down until you find the Apple Pencil option. Tapping it will take you to a page where you can manage stylus features such as Double Tap and Scribble. At the top of this page, you will also see your Apple Pencil's battery percentage.

ENTER TEXT WITH SCRIBBLE ON THE IPAD

Enabling Scribble

If it's not enabled already, go to the Settings menu, open Apple Pencil and toggle Scribble on:

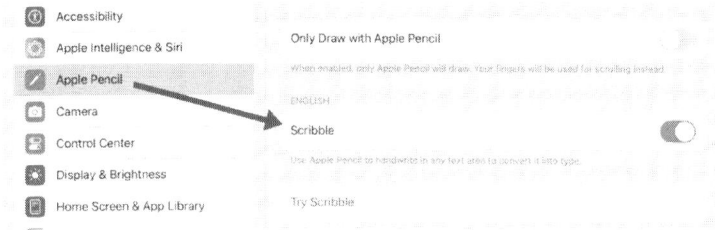

Accessibility

Apple Intelligence & Siri

Apple Pencil

Camera

Control Center

Display & Brightness

Home Screen & App Library

Only Draw with Apple Pencil

When enabled, only Apple Pencil will draw. Your fingers will be used for scrolling instead.

ENGLISH

Scribble

Use Apple Pencil to handwrite in any text area to convert it into type.

Try Scribble

Text Boxes

With Scribble enabled, you can now create a Text Box and write directly into the text field:

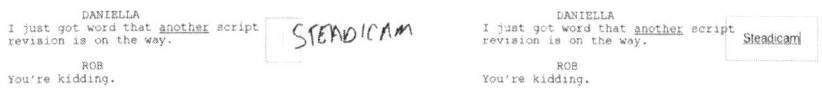

Sticky Notes

Scribble also works with Sticky Notes:

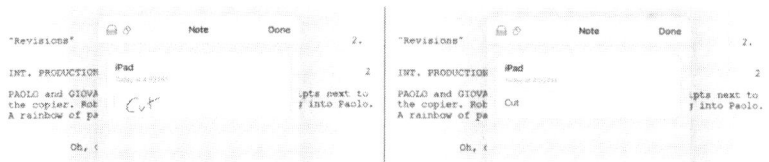

Scribble Toolbar

When you tap your Apple Pencil into any text field, the Scribble toolbar will be displayed at the bottom of the screen:

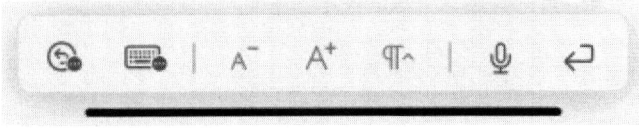

 With this toolbar, you can:

Undo / Redo actions
Display the mini-keyboard
Reduce or enlarge the text (touch the
Paragraph icon to show or hide the sizing
icons)
Turn on the dictation feature.
Insert a line break

HOW TO USE APPLE PENCIL TO ENTER TEXT IN ANY TEXT FIELD

Enabling Scribble

1. Open Settings on your iPad.

2. Tap Apple Pencil, then toggle Scribble to On.

3. (Optional) Tap Try Scribble in the same menu to practice gestures in a guided demo

Entering Text

- Direct Conversion: Write anywhere there's a text field, Messages, Safari, or form inputs, and you're handwriting instantly converts to typed text

- Edge-of-Field Writing: Scribble recognizes text even if you write beyond the visible boundary of the field

Editing Gestures

- Delete: Scratch out a word with a quick back-and-forth stroke

- Insert: Touch and hold at the insertion point until a space appears, then write to fill it

- Join/Split: Draw a vertical line between characters to merge or draw a separation to split them.

- Select: Circle text to select it or draw a line underneath to highlight; adjust selection handles as needed.

- Paragraph Selection: Triple-tap within a paragraph to select the entire block.

Scribble Toolbar & Shortcuts

A floating toolbar appears when you write, offering Undo, Show Keyboard, and other context-specific actions. Tap the ellipsis (...) to auto-minimize the toolbar and restore it with a single tap.

5.6 Integrations in Apple Apps

- Notes & Freeform: Tap the Markup icon, select Handwriting, and watch your notes convert as you write.

- Pages, Numbers & Keynote: Use Scribble to insert text directly into tables, shapes, and text boxes—no keyboard needed.

- Quick Note (iPadOS 15+): Swipe up from the bottom-right corner to open a Quick Note, write with Scribble, then paste the text into any app.

Tips & Best Practices

- Ergonomics: Lay the iPad flat, use a light grip on the Pencil, and rest your forearm on the table for comfort during long sessions.

- Language Support: Scribble adapts to the system language and supports multiple languages set in Settings > General > Keyboard.

- Gesture Mastery: Regularly revisit Settings > Apple Pencil > Try Scribble to sharpen your editing gestures.

HOW TO USE APPLE PENCIL TO ENTER TEXT IN NOTES AND FREEFORM

This section explains how to leverage Apple Pencil and the Scribble feature to handwrite directly in the Notes and Freeform apps on iPad—automatically converting your handwriting into editable text and offering intuitive editing gestures.

ENABLING SCRIBBLE

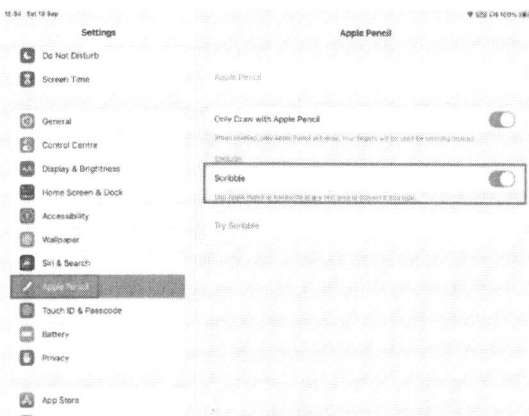

Before you begin, ensure Scribble is active:

1. Open Settings on your iPad.

2. Tap Apple Pencil, then turn Scribble On.

3. (Optional) Select Try Scribble to practice gestures like scratching out to delete or drawing a caret to insert text.

ENTERING AND EDITING TEXT IN NOTES

1. Open or create a note in the Notes app.

2. Tap the Markup switch off (pen-tip icon) to reveal the tool palette.

3. In the palette, tap the Handwriting tool (leftmost icon).

4. Write with Apple Pencil anywhere in the active area; Scribble converts your handwriting into typed text as you write.

5. Resize the writing area by dragging the Gray handle on the left edge up or down.

Key Editing Gestures in Notes

- Delete: Scratch through a word to remove it.

- Insert: Touch and hold between words until space appears, then write to fill it.

- Select: Circle text or underline it to select, then drag handles to adjust.

- Convert: Tap selected handwriting and choose Convert to switch it into editable typed text.

ENTERING AND EDITING TEXT IN FREEFORM

1. Launch Freeform and open or create a board.

2. Tap the Markup Switch off (pen-tip icon) to display drawing tools.

3. Select the Handwriting tool from the palette.

4. Write anywhere on the canvas; your handwriting is rendered as smooth, vector-based text objects you can move, resize, or recolour.

Smart Selection in Freeform

- Use the Lasso tool to circle handwriting; once selected, you can Copy as Text, Cut, Delete, or Group strokes with sticky notes.

- Freeform boards sync via iCloud, so converted or selected text updates in real time for collaborators.

HOW TO CHOOSE TEXT AND CHANGE IT WITH APPLE PENCIL

Getting Started with Markup

Before diving into text selection and editing, open any supported app (Notes, Photos, Mail, Files, or any PDF reader), then tap the Markup button (usually a pen tip icon) to reveal the Markup toolbar at the bottom of the screen.

If the toolbar is hidden, tap the minimized Show Handwriting Tools button to expand it.

Selecting Content with the Lasso Tool

- In the Markup toolbar, choose the Lasso tool (it sits between the eraser and the ruler).

- Select a word or drawn object by double-tapping it with your Apple Pencil.

- Select a sentence by triple-tapping anywhere within it.

- Select a paragraph or block of handwriting by touching and holding at the start, then dragging to the end. For finer control, drag slowly to adjust the selection boundary.

- Select multiple objects (shapes, drawings, or handwriting) by drawing a free-form loop around them.

Editing Handwritten Annotations

Once selected, tapped-in content lifts slightly:

- Move it by dragging to a new location.

- Cut, copy, delete, and duplicate via the contextual menu that appears.

- Change colour by tapping a new colour swatch in the Markup toolbar.

To erase mistakes in drawings or handwriting, switch to the Eraser tool:

- Pixel Eraser scrubs away individual strokes.

- Object Eraser removes entire selected shapes or handwriting in one tap.

Adding and Editing Typed Text Boxes

1. In the Markup toolbar, tap the Add Annotation ("+") button, then choose Add Text.

2. A text box appears, tap inside it, and enter text via the on-screen keyboard or an external keyboard.

3. Tap outside the box to commit your text, or drag its blue handles to resize the box.

To reopen and edit that text box later:

- Tap it once to reveal the cursor, then type or delete as needed.

Formatting Text Boxes

With a text box selected, the bottom of the Markup toolbar shows formatting controls:

- Font & Size dropdown lets you pick typeface and adjust size.

- Justification (left, centre, right) aligns the text within the box.

- Style options for bold, italics, and underline transform your text with a tap.

- Colour picker changes text colour; tap Grid, Spectrum, or Sliders for custom hues.

Working in Pages and Notes

- **Pages:** After entering Markup, you can both annotate and insert text boxes in any document. Use the Lasso to select annotations, then move or style them as needed.

- **Notes:** Tap Markup, select the Handwriting Tools, then write or draw freely. You can mix handwriting with typed text boxes seamlessly. For heading styles, double-tap a word or triple-tap a block, then choose Title or Heading from the Aa formatting menu.

Advanced Tools: Ruler & Undo

- **Ruler:** Tap the ruler icon, draw straight lines along its edge, then reposition or rotate with two fingers. Hide it by tapping the icon again.

- **Undo/Redo:** Quickly revert changes with the curved arrow buttons at the top of the Markup toolbar.

Best Practices

- Practice in Freeform or on a new note to build muscle memory for selections and edits.

- Use Zoom: Pinch to zoom into dense areas before selecting small handwriting.

- Maintain contrast: Ensure your text box colour contrasts with the background for readability.

- Combine tools: Start with Lasso selection, then switch to Eraser or Move to refine specific strokes.

By mastering these Markup tools with your Apple Pencil, you'll elevate how you select, edit, and format both handwriting and text on your iPad, turning every annotation into a polished, professional result.

HOW TO STOP CONVERTING YOUR HANDWRITING TO TEXT

Disabling the automatic conversion of handwriting into text on your iPad requires turning off the Scribble feature in the Apple Pencil settings and ensuring that freehand drawing remains active. Scribble can be toggled off in a few taps within **Settings > Apple Pencil**, and you can further refine your experience by enabling **Only Draw with Apple Pencil** so that your stylus only produces handwriting or drawings and never summons text input modes. After adjusting these settings, verify the change in native apps like Notes and Pages, and explore app-specific drawing or markup tools to maintain pure handwriting.

1. Open Apple Pencil Settings

First, unlock your iPad and tap the **Settings** icon to access system-wide preferences.
Scroll down the left sidebar until you find **Apple Pencil**, then tap to open the Apple Pencil configuration pane.
Here you will see options for "Scribble" and "Only Draw with Apple Pencil."

2. Turn Off Scribble

Locate the **Scribble** toggle near the top of the Apple Pencil settings.
Tap the switch so that it moves to the **Off** position, indicated by a gray background. Once off, the iPad will no longer convert your handwriting into typed text across any app.

3. Enable Only Draw with Apple Pencil

Directly below Scribble, find **Only Draw with Apple Pencil** and tap its toggle to **On**. This setting ensures that finger touches won't create strokes and that the Pencil exclusively produces freehand input. With both Scribble disabled and Only Draw enabled, your Pencil becomes a pure drawing tool.

4. Verify in Notes App

Launch the **Notes** app from your Home Screen to confirm behaviour.
Open an existing note or create a new one, then tap the **pen tip** icon to enter Markup or Drawing mode. Try writing with the Apple Pencil—your handwriting should now remain exactly as drawn, without converting to text.

5. Check Pages and Other Apps

Open **Pages**, tap the **pen tip** icon to enter annotation mode, and draft freehand text; it should stay as handwriting. In **Freeform**, Photos, or any PDF reader supporting Markup, select the drawing tool and write—none of your strokes will auto-convert.

If any app still converts handwriting, revisit **Settings** > **Apple Pencil** to reconfirm Scribble is off.

6. Restart iPad If Needed

Occasionally, changes in Pencil behaviour require an iPad reboot to fully apply. Press and hold the top button and either volume button, slide to power off, wait 30 seconds, then hold the top button to restart. After rebooting, test your handwriting again to confirm Scribble remains disabled.

7. App-Specific Tips

Some third-party apps may have their handwriting conversion settings—check within their in-app preferences.

For example, in GoodNotes, tap the Pen tool twice, open **Pen Gestures**, and disable "Scribble to Erase" if you prefer manual erasing.

If you use OneNote, disable its ink-to-text feature under **Draw > Ink to Text** in the app's ribbon.

8. Best Practices

Practice drawing and handwriting in **Freeform** to build muscle memory without interference from auto-conversion.

Use **Zoom** (pinch gesture) when writing small annotations to ensure accuracy and avoid stray strokes being misinterpreted.

Regularly update iPadOS via **Settings** > **General** > **Software Update** to benefit from the latest Apple Pencil improvements.

By following these steps, your iPad will no longer transform your handwriting into text unless you explicitly choose to re-enable that feature, giving you full control over when and how your Apple Pencil input is interpreted.

HOW TO DRAW WITH APPLE PENCIL ON IPAD

Learning to create digital artwork on an iPad can introduce exciting new possibilities for both aspiring and professional creatives. When used alongside an Apple Pencil, the iPad becomes a powerful tool for drawing and design, with many additional capabilities beyond simple sketching.

This beginner-friendly guide walks you through the key steps to get started. You'll learn how to pair your Apple Pencil, choose suitable drawing apps, and make the most of the stylus in your creative process. The guide also includes practice activities to help you gradually improve your digital art skills.

If you're still deciding which device to use, take a look at our recommendations for top iPads designed for artists as well as other popular drawing tablets.

Once you're set up and ready, continue reading to discover how to begin drawing on your iPad.

The Apple Pencil (2nd generation) attaches securely to the iPad using the magnetic strip along one of the tablet's longer edges.

HOW TO DRAW ON THE IPAD: PAIR YOUR APPLE PENCIL.

Before you begin drawing on your iPad, the first step is to connect your Apple Pencil to the device. Thankfully, the process is straightforward and works smoothly regardless of which Apple Pencil model you're using.

To connect the first-generation Apple Pencil, start by taking off the rounded cap at the end of the stylus. This will uncover the built-in Lightning connector. Insert the connector into your iPad's Lightning port. Once it's plugged in, a prompt should appear on the screen with a "Pair" button. Tap that button, and your Apple Pencil will be ready to use.

To connect the second-generation Apple Pencil(Pro) to a compatible iPad, simply place the stylus on the magnetic connector located along the right edge of the device. Before doing this, make sure Bluetooth is enabled in your iPad's settings. Once the Apple Pencil attaches magnetically, it will pair automatically with your iPad. This same connection point also serves as the charging area, so your stylus will begin charging as soon as it's connected.

Drawing on the iPad: Which apps to use

Creating simple sketches is easy using the built-in Notes app, which makes it a great starting point for learning the basics of digital drawing.

If your goal is simply to begin sketching, your iPad already has everything you need. Apps like Notes and Pages come preinstalled and include a selection of basic tools such as pens and colour options, allowing you to start drawing right away. These apps help get familiar with how the Apple Pencil feels and responds. However, they do not offer the advanced features and creative flexibility found in professional drawing apps like Procreate, ArtRage, or Affinity Designer.

Five of the best iPad drawing apps:

Procreate – A powerful painting app that supports both 2D and 3D artwork, delivering professional-level results.
• **Adobe Illustrator** – A leading vector design application widely used in creative industries.
• **Linea Sketch** – A sketching app for iPad that

offers a freemium model with essential tools.
• **Affinity Designer** – A feature-rich design platform suitable for branding, illustration, and digital   art.
• **Autodesk Sketchbook** – A user-friendly drawing app that is ideal for beginners and experienced artists alike.

There is a wide selection of excellent drawing apps available for the iPad, including both free and paid options. We've highlighted some of the top choices in our guide to the best iPad drawing apps, where you can explore more possibilities. Among these, Procreate stands out as one of the most popular choices, and we also offer a separate guide to help you choose the best iPad for using Procreate effectively.

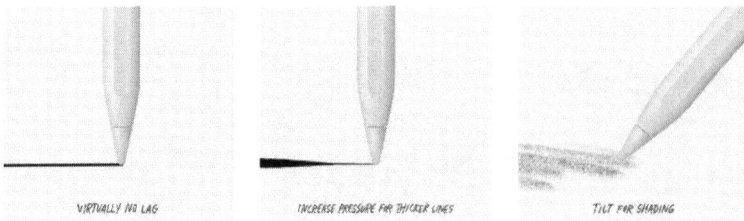

VIRTUALLY NO LAG   INCREASE PRESSURE FOR THICKER LINES   TILT FOR SHADING

The iPad allows you to take advantage of pressure sensitivity, enabling you to draw lines that vary in thickness depending on how hard you press with the Apple Pencil. This is one of the key features of the stylus, though it may take some time to become comfortable using it effectively.

The best way to get a feel for how pressure sensitivity works is through regular practice. Open your preferred drawing app, or simply use the built-in Notes app, and begin testing how different levels of pressure affect your strokes. Try to observe the range between the lightest and heaviest lines you can create, and explore the subtle variations in between.

The goal is to develop an intuitive understanding of how pressure impacts your drawing. With time, you'll begin to recognize how different levels of force translate into specific line qualities, helping you gain more control and precision in your digital artwork.

Understand palm rejection on the iPad.

One aspect that may take some time to adjust to when drawing on an iPad is the built-in palm rejection feature. This technology allows you to rest your hand directly on the screen while working, so you don't need to awkwardly hold your hand in the air as you draw.

Many beginners or those new to digital drawing on the iPad often try to avoid touching the screen with their hand, unsure if it might interfere with their work. However, once you become familiar with palm rejection, you'll realize that the iPad is designed to ignore unintended touches from your hand.

Embracing this feature lets you draw more naturally and comfortably, much like you would on a sheet of paper. It makes the entire experience more fluid, intuitive, and less physically straining.

Practice tilt sensitivity for drawing on iPad

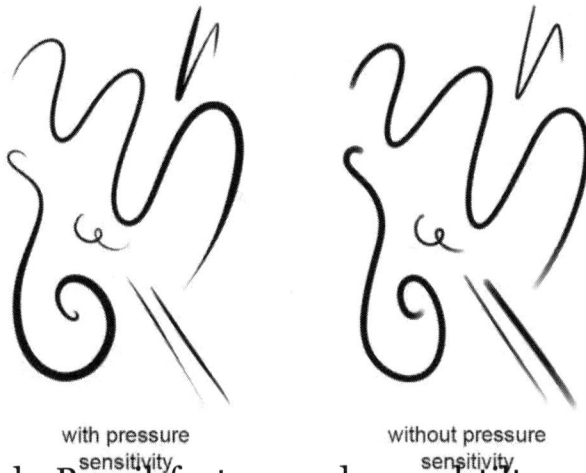

with pressure sensitivity.

without pressure sensitivity.

The Apple Pencil features advanced tilt sensitivity, which gives you greater control over the appearance and style of your lines. The iPad can detect the angle at which you hold the stylus, as well as the part of the tip that makes contact with the screen.

For example, holding the Pencil in an upright position allows you to draw very thin, precise lines. Tilting it to the side enables you to produce broader, softer strokes. This feature is especially useful for adding shading and depth to your artwork.

To become familiar with tilt sensitivity, open a drawing app and spend some time practicing with different brushes and tools. Try varying the angle of the Pencil to see the kinds of textures and effects you can create. This hands-on approach will help you understand how tilt influences your strokes and how you can use it to enhance your digital illustrations.

Apple Pencil practice exercises for learning how to draw on the iPad

Doing simple practice exercises is a great way to become more comfortable with drawing on the iPad using the Apple Pencil. Since every artist has a unique approach, the best way to improve your skills will vary from person to person. Still, here are a few helpful Apple Pencil exercises that can guide you as you develop better technique and control.

Drawing lines: Make it a habit to practice basic strokes regularly. Open a blank canvas in the Notes app or your preferred drawing app and try drawing horizontal lines close together without letting them touch. Repeat the process with vertical lines, then move on to curved lines. For an added challenge, try going back and drawing another set of lines between the ones you've already made. You can also experiment with dashed lines, focusing on keeping the spacing and length as consistent as possible.

Tracing and copying: The Apple Pencil is highly precise, and you can even use it to trace through a sheet of paper placed over your iPad screen. While this won't work with thick paper or cardboard, standard paper or thinner materials usually work well. Lay the sheet on top of your iPad and carefully trace the lines with the stylus.

You can also practice by copying images directly from your iPad. If your device has a large enough screen, you can open a reference image in the Photos app and position it on one side of the screen. On the other side, launch your drawing app and try to replicate the image.

Calligraphy: Practicing calligraphy is another excellent way to improve your control and precision with the Apple Pencil. It also works well as a short daily exercise. You can choose one of your Favorite fonts, display it on your screen, and try to recreate the lettering by hand using your stylus. This not only builds consistency but also helps with stroke discipline and attention to detail.

How to use the Apple Pencil Pro's double-tap for drawing on the iPad

If you're using the more advanced second-generation Apple Pencil, be sure to take advantage of a useful built-in feature: the double-tap. Unlike the original Apple Pencil, which lacks physical controls, the second-generation model allows you to tap twice on the flat edge of the stylus to quickly switch between tools or settings.

Once you get into the habit of using this gesture, it can become a very convenient way to speed up your workflow and make drawing more efficient.

These are the settings available for the double-tap:

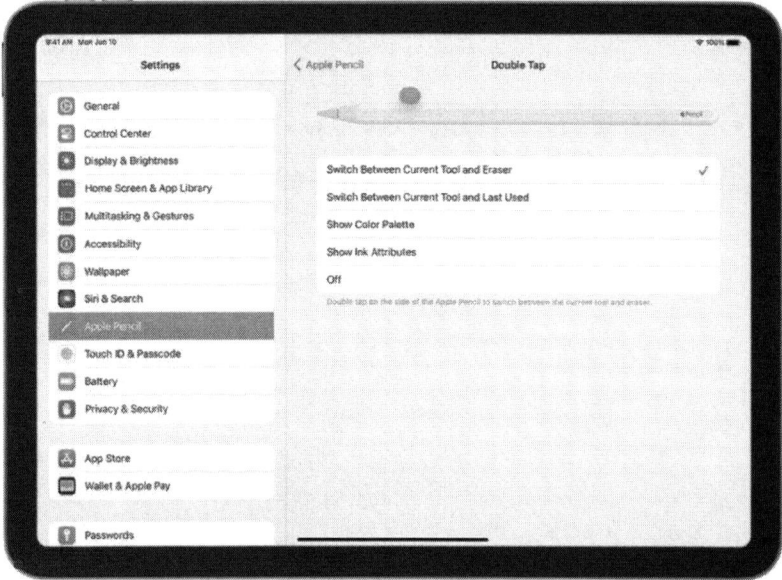

- Switch between your current tool and the eraser (this is the default setting).
  • Toggle between the current tool and the one you used previously.
  • Open the colour palette.
  • Disable the double-tap function entirely.
- As you can see, getting started with drawing on an iPad is simple. You don't need advanced software or technical experience, just your iPad, your Apple Pencil, and a willingness to explore and experiment.
- Using the iPad for drawing feels natural and user-friendly. It also supports traditional drawing principles, so you can apply common

techniques such as those found in guides for sketching animals, people, and landscapes. Try these classic approaches with the drawing apps we've suggested and use the iPad's built-in technology to create impressive digital artwork.

- If you're interested in other options beyond the iPad, take a look at our recommendations for the best drawing tablets for students and the best drawing tablets for kids. These guides include a variety of brands in addition to Apple products.

HOW TO APPLY SHADING AND DARKER LINES

1. Pressure Sensitivity

What it does:

- Press harder to make your strokes darker and bolder.

- Lighten your touch for faint, delicate lines.

Why it matters:

- Varying line weight instantly adds depth, volume, and expressiveness to sketches and lettering.

2. Tilt Shading

How to use it:

- Tilt the pencil on its side to engage the flat "edge" of brushes like Watercolour, Graphite, Charcoal, or the Chisel Marker.

- Sweep broadly for soft fills or deep, painterly strokes.

Pro Tip:

- Lower the brush opacity via the Pen toolbar for even gentler gradients and subtle blending.

3. Azimuth (Rotation)

What you'll see:

- With the Chisel Marker selected, twist the pencil in your fingers and watch the stroke direction pivot in real time, just like a real marker tip!

4. Consistent Mechanical Lines

When to use it:

- For technical drawings, calligraphy, or any time you need a uniform, unwavering stroke.

How it works:

- Select the Technical Pen brush. Your line width and opacity stay fixed, regardless of pressure or tilt.

- To adjust thickness, simply pick a different pen size.

5. Quick Tool-Switching (Double-Tap)

Setup:

1. In **iPad Settings** > **Apple Pencil**, enable "Double-Tap."

2. In Procreate **Preferences** > **Gesture Controls**, turn on **Custom Double-Tap Behaviour**.

How to switch:

- Double-tap near the tip of your Pencil 2 to cycle through brushes, eraser, smudge tool, or your last-used tools.

Important:

- Turning on Custom Double-Tap in Procreate overrides the system-wide Pencil setting.

- If you want double-tap specifically to toggle the eraser, disable Custom Double-Tap in Procreate, then in **iPad Settings** > **Apple Pencil**, choose "Switch Between Current Tool and Eraser."

6. Hover Preview

What it does:

- As you hover your Apple Pencil (iPad Pro 2022 or newer), Procreate shows a live preview of where your next stroke will land.

Why it helps:

- Perfect for ultra-precise placement before you commit ink to the canvas.

HOW TO DOUBLE-TAP TO SWITCH TOOLS

System-Wide Configuration

1. **Select Apple Pencil**: Scroll down the left sidebar and tap Apple Pencil.

2. **Tap Double Tap**: Under the Pencil menu, choose Double Tap. You'll see five options.

3. **Choose Your Action:**

   o Switch Between Current Tool and Eraser (default)

   o Switch Between Current Tool and Last Used Tool

   o Show Colour Palette

   o Show Ink Attributes (brush size, opacity sliders)

   o Off (disable double-tap entirely)

4. **Enable Hover-Only (Optional):** Toggle Allow Double Tap Only with Hover to restrict the gesture to when your Pencil hovers just above the screen— useful for avoiding accidental taps during fast strokes.

5. App-Specific Overrides (Procreate Example)

Many creative apps let you override the system gesture so you can assign even more tailored shortcuts.

1. Open Procreate and tap the Actions (wrench) icon in the top toolbar.

2. Choose Gesture Controls ▶ Apple Pencil.

3. Toggle on Custom Double-Tap Behaviour to enable Procreate's shortcuts.

4. Assign Tools: Select any two functions to swap—commonly Brush ↔ Eraser, Brush ↔ Smudge, or Brush ↔ Last Used

5. Remember: While Procreate's custom setting is active, the system setting under Settings ▶ Apple Pencil is ignored until you disable the override.

Troubleshooting Tips

- Bluetooth Connection: Double-tap requires an active Bluetooth link. If options vanish or the gesture stops, confirm Bluetooth is on and your Pencil is paired under Settings ▶ Bluetooth.

- Supported Hardware: Only Apple Pencil (2nd gen) and Apple Pencil Pro feature double-tap; the USB-C Pencil does not support it.

- App Compatibility: Not all apps implement double-tap. While Notes, Procreate, and Adobe Fresco embrace it, some niche or older apps may not.

- Accessibility Settings: An alternate toggle lives in Settings ▶ Accessibility ▶ Apple Pencil, where you can adjust double-tap timing or disable it for users needing a slower gesture window.

Pro Tips for Smooth Workflows

- Dedicated Eraser Swap: To reserve double-tap exclusively for erasing, disable app overrides, and choose Switch Between Current Tool and Eraser in system settings.

- Colour-Switch Shortcut: Map double-tap to show Colour Palette if you frequently change hues mid-drawing—no more diving into menus.

- Combine with Hover Preview: On 2022+ iPad Pro models, enable Brush Cursor or similar hover-preview options in your app to see a live stroke outline before you touch—pair that with double-tap and tool placement becomes a dance of speed and precision.

- Stay Updated: Keep your iPadOS and Pencil firmware current—unexpected bugs in older versions can disrupt gesture recognition.

With your Apple Pencil Pro properly tuned—system double-tap, app overrides, and hover settings—you'll cycle through brushes, erasers, swatches, and more in an instant, letting your creativity flow uninterrupted from thought to stroke.

HOW TO SQUEEZE APPLE PENCIL PRO TO PERFORM ACTION

Accessing the Squeeze Menu

- Open Settings on your iPad.

- Scroll down and tap Apple Pencil.

- Tap Squeeze to enter the Squeeze configuration screen.

Choosing Your Squeeze Action

On the Squeeze screen, you'll see a list of available actions. Tap your preferred one:

Action	What It Does
Switch to Eraser	Hold the squeeze to erase; release to revert to your previous tool.
Switch to Last Used Tool	Hold the squeeze to use your last active tool; release to return.
Show Colour Palette	Single squeeze & release opens the colour picker; choose swatches, then it auto-closes.
Show Tool Palette/Picker	Opens the full tool selector (brushes, pens, shapes, etc.).
Run a Shortcut	Assign any iOS Shortcut— e.g., insert a template, sign a document, or toggle Dark Mode.
Off	Disables all squeeze functionality.

HOW TO TURN HAPTIC FEEDBACK FOR APPLE PENCIL PRO OFF OR ON

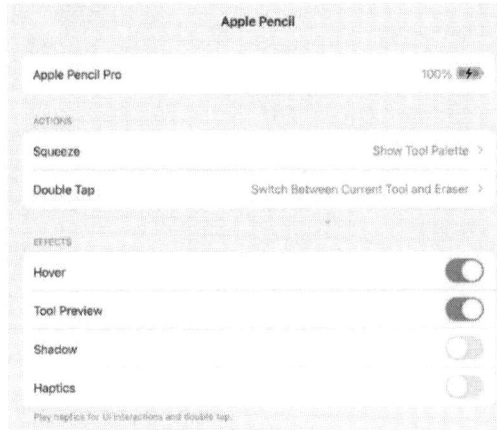

1. Basic On/Off in iPadOS Settings

1. Open Settings on your iPad.

2. Scroll down and tap Apple Pencil in the sidebar.

3. Locate the Haptics toggle:

   o On: Enables the internal vibration motor for tactile feedback as you draw.

   o Off: Disables all haptic feedback from the pencil.

2. Verifying Hardware Compatibility

- Apple Pencil Pro only: Haptic feedback is unique to the Pencil Pro model and requires a compatible iPad Pro (M4) or newer.

- No haptics on USB-C Pencil: The entry-level USB-C Apple Pencil lacks haptic motors and gesture zones

3. Accessibility Panel Controls

If you still don't see the Haptics toggle, or if haptics won't respond:

1. Go to Settings ▶ Accessibility ▶ Apple Pencil.

2. Here you'll find:

   o Turn Haptics On/Off (mirror of the main setting).

   o Squeeze Sensitivity slider (for the squeeze gesture, but may affect haptic responsiveness).

   o Double-Tap On/Off with duration controls (separate from haptics).

4. Troubleshooting Steps

- Bluetooth Connection: Ensure your Pencil Pro is paired and Bluetooth is active under Settings ▶ Bluetooth; without it, haptics won't function.

- Restart & Re-pair: If toggling settings doesn't work, restart your iPad and re-pair the Pencil via Settings ▶ Apple Pencil.

- Software Update: Confirm you're on iPadOS 18 or newer—haptic support for Pencil Pro was added in this release.

5. In-App Behaviour: Final Cut Pro for iPad Example

Some apps expose their haptic toggle or rely on system settings:

- In Final Cut Pro for iPad, you can enable or disable haptic feedback for editing tasks under Settings ▶ Apple Pencil ▶ Haptics—mirroring the system switch.

HOVER TO PREVIEW TOOLS AND CONTROLS

1. Enabling or Disabling Hover Preview

1. Open Settings: Tap the Settings app on your iPad.

2. Select Apple Pencil: Scroll down the left sidebar and choose Apple Pencil.

3. Toggle Hover: Find Hover (sometimes labelled "Preview tools and controls") and flip the switch on to show a live brush cursor while hovering, or off to disable the feature.

2. What Hover Allows You to Do

With Hover enabled, holding your Apple Pencil up to 12 mm above the screen displays a live preview of where and how your next mark, tool selection, or eraser action will land:

- Tool Palette Preview: Hover over brush, eraser, colour, or shape icons to see expanded tool options before touching.

- Stroke Preview: In drawing apps (Notes, GoodNotes, procreate 5.3+, etc.), see the forthcoming stroke's shape, thickness, and opacity in real time.

- Barrel Roll Preview: On Apple Pencil Pro, rotate the barrel (azimuth) while hovering to preview angled brushes like the highlighter or fountain pen.

- Precision Erasing: Select the eraser tool, hover to choose pixel or object eraser sizes, and position the eraser exactly where you need it.

3. App-Level Overrides

Some apps provide their Hover settings or rely on system defaults:

- Procreate: In Procreate 5.3+, enable Actions ▶ Preferences ▶ Brush Cursor to turn on the hover preview for brushes and smudges.

- GoodNotes: Hover must be enabled in Settings ▶ Apple Pencil, then GoodNotes will show stroke and tool icon previews automatically.

- Other Apps: Check each app's settings—while many Apple Pencil-aware apps support Hover, some niche apps may not implement it yet.

4. Troubleshooting Hover Issues

If you don't see Hover working as expected:

1. Verify Hardware/OS: Confirm you're on a supported iPad + Pencil and iPadOS 16.1+.

2. Check Settings: Make sure Settings ▶ Apple Pencil ▶ Hover is toggled On.

3. Restart & Re-pair: Toggle Bluetooth off/on in Settings ▶ Bluetooth, restart your iPad, and re-pair your Apple Pencil under Settings ▶ Apple Pencil.

4. Update Apps: Ensure your drawing app is updated to the latest version—some Hover features arrive in app updates rather than system updates.

HOW TO TAKE AND MARK UP A SCREENSHOT WITH APPLE PENCIL ON IPAD

Method A: Corner-Swipe Gesture

1. **Position Your Pencil**
   Place the tip in either bottom corner of the screen
   (left or right).

2. **Swipe Diagonally**
   Drag your Pencil in a quick diagonal motion
   toward the centre. This instantly captures the
   current screen.

3. **Enter Markup Mode**
   The screenshot preview appears immediately.
   Use your Pencil to:

   - Draw or write freehand

   - Highlight text or areas

   - Add shapes, arrows, or callouts

4. **Save or Share**
   Tap **Done**, then choose **Save to Photos**, **Files**,
   or **Share** via any app.

Method B: Assistive Touch Button

1. **Enable Assistive Touch**
   Go to **Settings** ▶ **Accessibility** ▶ **Touch** ▶ **Assistive Touch** and turn it on.

2. **Customize Top-Level Menu**
   Tap **Customize Top Level Menu** ▶ +, then add **Screenshot**.

3. **Capture with Your Pencil**
   Tap the floating Assistive Touch button with your Pencil to take a screenshot. You'll immediately enter the same markup interface as above.

4. **Quick Tips**

   - **Fast Annotations**: In markup mode, choose a highlighter or fine-tip brush for quick notes.

   - **Undo/Redo**: Tap with two fingers to undo; three fingers to redo.

   - **Adjust Stroke**: Use the slider on the side of the markup toolbar to change pen thickness or opacity.

- **Share Templates**: If you often annotate similar layouts (e.g., lesson plans, forms), save blank templates in Photos and reuse them.

CHAPTER THREE:

CREATE QUICK NOTES ANYWHERE ON THE IPAD

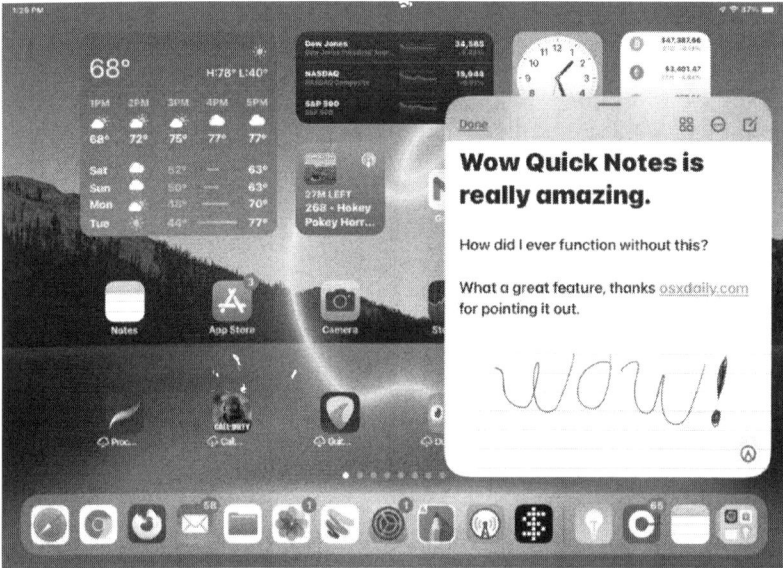

Corner-Swipe Gesture

Enable Corner Gestures

- Open Settings ▶ Notes ▶ Quick Notes.

- Tap Corner Gestures and turn it on.

- Assign Bottom Right (or left) to Quick Note.

Create a Quick Note

- From anywhere on your iPad, touch the bottom-right corner with your Apple Pencil Pro.

- Swipe toward the center of the screen.

- A Quick Note window appears—jot, draw, or sketch instantly.

Save & Exit

- Tap Done when finished; your note is saved in Notes ▶ Quick Notes.

Control Centre Shortcut

1. Add Quick Note to Control Center

   - Go to Settings ▶ Control Center.

   - Tap Customize Controls, then tap + next to Quick Note.

Invoke Quick Note

- Swipe down from the top-right corner to open Control Center.

- Tap the Quick Note icon.

- Write or draw; tap Done to save.

Keyboard Shortcuts (External Keyboards)

1. Globe + Q

   o With a compatible external keyboard connected, press Globe + Q to open a new Quick Note.

2. Command + N

   o If a Quick Note is already visible, press ⌘ + N to start another new Quick Note.

Lock-Screen Tap

1. Enable Lock Screen Access

   o Navigate to Settings ▶ Notes ▶ Access Notes from Lock Screen.

   o Select Always Create Quick Note (or your preferred option).

2. Take a Quick Note from Lock Screen

   o With your iPad locked, tap anywhere on the lock screen using your Apple Pencil Pro.

- A Quick Note pops up instantly; write or sketch.

- Tap Done to lock your note into the Quick Notes folder.

Viewing & Organizing Quick Notes

1. Open the Notes App

- In the sidebar, tap Quick Notes to see everything you've captured.

2. Convert to Standard Notes

- To lock or move a Quick Note out of that folder, drag it into another folder, then it behaves like any regular note.

Add Links & Tags

- Inside a Quick Note, you can tap Add Link when viewing content (e.g., Safari or Calendar) to automatically include context.

- Use Tags in the note body to organize them by project or topic.

HOW TO MAKE A QUICK NOTE

1. Invoke Quick Note

- Place your Apple Pencil at the bottom-right corner of the iPad screen.

- Swipe up toward the center.

2. Start Writing or Drawing

- A floating Quick Note window appears with a "Get Started" button.

- Tap Get Started to open the canvas.

○ Use your Pencil to jot down text, sketch, or scribble your ideas.

3. Save Your Note

○ When you're done, tap Done.

○ Your Quick Note is automatically saved.

HOW TO REOPEN OR LINK BACK TO A QUICK NOTE

- **Reopen**: From anywhere—whether you're in Safari, Mail, or any other app—just swipe up again from the bottom-right corner with your Apple Pencil. Your most recent Quick Note will reappear for additional edits or reference.

- **Add Links:** While editing, you can include links back to the original content (web pages, documents, etc.) so that tapping them later returns you to the context that inspired the note.

WHERE TO FIND ALL YOUR QUICK NOTES

- Open the Notes App: In the sidebar, tap Quick Notes to see every Quick Note you've captured.

- From there, you can browse, organize, or convert any Quick Note into a full-size note in any folder you choose

HOW TO VIEW AND ORGANIZE QUICK NOTES

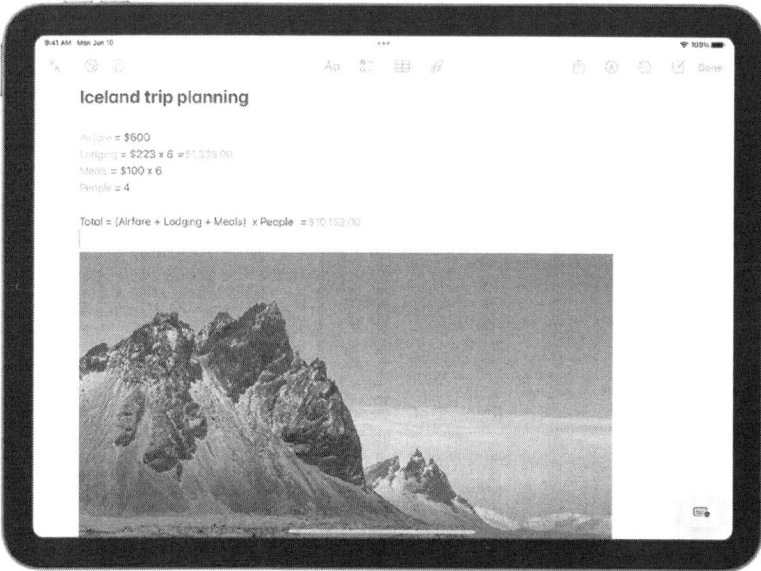

1. Minimize Your Quick Note

- After you finish and tap Done, your Quick Note doesn't vanish—it becomes a floating thumbnail in the corner.

- Swipe the thumbnail sideways to tuck it anywhere along the edge.

2. Reopen the Floating Note

- Swipe up from the bottom-right corner to summon Quick Note.

- Swipe over to the corner where you parked the thumbnail and tap it to expand your note.

3. Find All Quick Notes in the Notes App

- Open the Notes app.

- Tap the sidebar icon (top-left) if the folder list isn't visible.

- Under Folders, select Quick Notes.

- You'll see every Quick Note you've created—tap one (for example, "Hello") to open it full-screen.

HOW TO CHANGE OR DISABLE THE CORNER GESTURE FOR QUICK NOTES.

How to Change or Disable Quick Note Corner Gestures on iPad

🔧 Adjust Corner Gestures via Notes Settings

1. Open the Settings app on your iPad.

2. Scroll down and tap Notes.

3. Select Corner Gestures.

4. Here, you can customize the actions for each corner:

   - Tap the Left Corner Swipe or the Right Corner Swipe.

   - Choose an action: Quick Note, Screenshot, or Off to disable the gesture.

5. To prevent accidental activation with your finger, toggle off Allow Finger to Swipe from Corner.

This method allows you to tailor the corner gestures to your preference or disable them entirely.

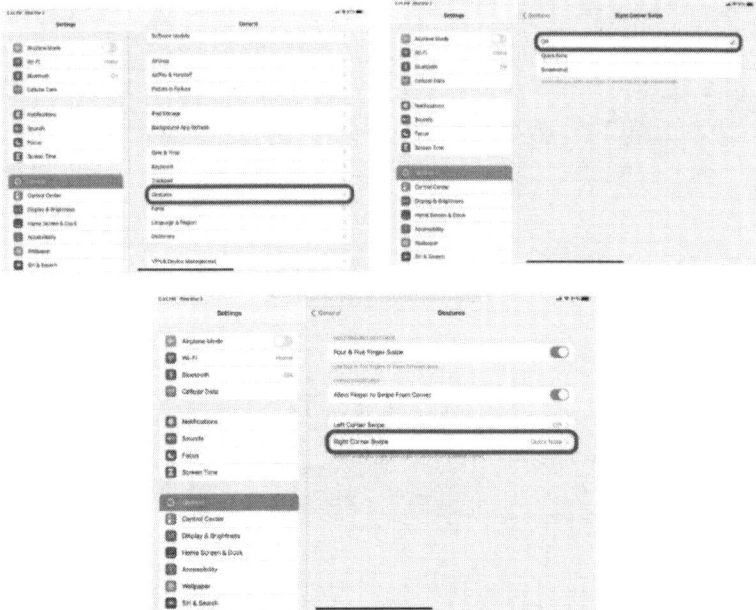

✏️ Modify Apple Pencil Gestures

If you're using an Apple Pencil and wish to adjust its corner gestures:

1. Open the Settings app.

2. Tap Apple Pencil.

3. Under Pencil Gestures, select Left Corner Swipe or Right Corner Swipe.

4. Choose your desired action: Quick Note, Screenshot, or Off. This customization ensures that your Apple Pencil behaves as you prefer when interacting with screen corners.

⚠ Important Considerations

- **Finger Gestures:** Disabling finger-based corner gestures requires turning off the Allow Finger to Swipe from Corner option in the Notes settings.

- **Stage Manager:** If you're unable to toggle off corner gestures, ensure that Stage Manager is disabled, as it may interfere with gesture settings.

- **Note Access**: Disabling corner gestures doesn't delete your existing Quick Notes. You can still access them in the Quick Notes folder within the Notes app.

CHAPTER FOUR:

DO MORE WITH THE APPLE PENCIL PRO

WRITE A QUICK NOTE

✍ Creating a Quick Note

To create a Quick Note from any app:

- **Swipe up from the bottom right corner** of the display using your Apple Pencil Pro.

This gesture opens a new Quick Note where you can start writing immediately.

📇 Adding Content to a Quick Note

In a Quick Note, you can:

- **Add links**: Tap the Share button in an app and select "Add to Quick Note."

- **Insert images**: Drag and drop images into the note.

- **Use tags and mentions**: Organize your notes with hashtags or mention contacts for easy reference.

📁 Accessing Your Quick Notes

All your Quick Notes are saved in the Notes app:

1. Open the **Notes** app on your iPad.

2. Tap on the **Quick Notes** folder in the folders list.

Here, you can view and organize all your Quick Notes.

🔄 Syncing Across Devices

When you create a Quick Note on your iPad, it syncs across your Apple devices. You can access and edit your Quick Notes on your iPhone and Mac, ensuring your notes are always up to date.

GATHER IDEAS IN FREEFORM

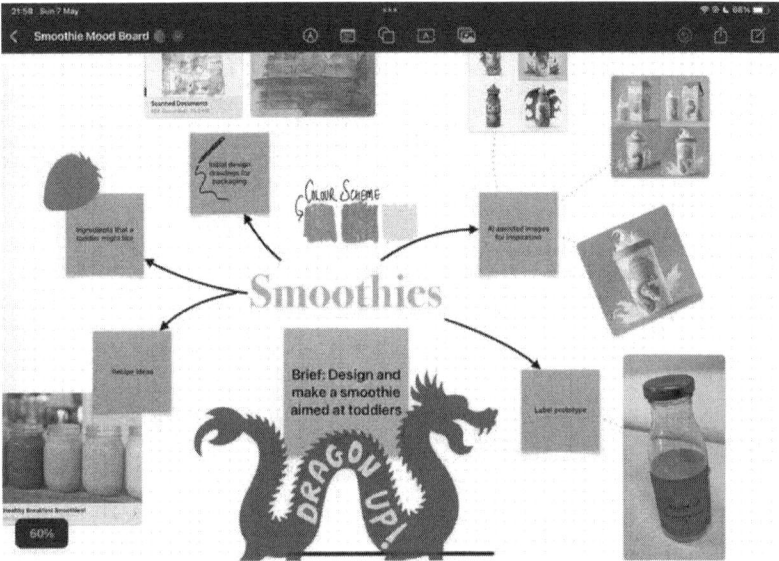

Create or Open a Board

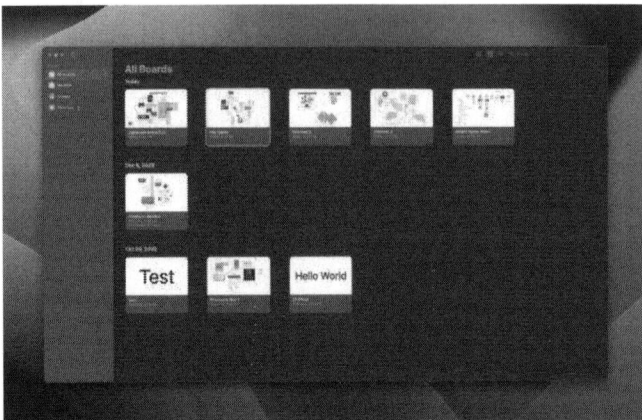

Launch the Freeform app and tap the "+" button to start a new board, or select an existing one to continue your work. Freeform offers an infinite canvas, allowing you to expand your workspace as needed.

2. Enable iCloud Sync

Ensure your boards are saved and accessible across all your Apple devices by enabling iCloud for Freeform: Go to Settings > [Your Name] > iCloud > Show All, then toggle on Freeform.

✏️ Utilizing Apple Pencil Pro Features

The Apple Pencil Pro introduces advanced functionalities to enhance your creative process in Freeform:

Pressure Sensitivity

Apply varying pressure to create lines of different thicknesses, adding depth and emphasis to your drawings.

Tilt Sensitivity

Tilt the pencil to adjust the shape and angle of your strokes, enabling shading and dynamic brush effects.

Squeeze Gesture

Gently squeeze the barrel of the Apple Pencil Pro to quickly access the tool palette or switch between tools. You can customize this action by navigating to Settings > Apple Pencil > Squeeze.

Barrel Roll

Rotate the pencil to change the orientation of certain tools, such as the highlighter or fountain pen, allowing for precise control over stroke angles.

🔧 Leveraging Freeform's Tools

Drawing and Handwriting

Tap the Drawing Tools button or simply start using your Apple Pencil Pro to draw. You can adjust line thickness, opacity, and colour to suit your creative needs.

Adding Sticky Notes

Insert sticky notes to jot down quick ideas, create to-do lists, or provide feedback. Customize their colour and resize them as needed.

Inserting Files and Media

Enhance your board by adding documents, images, videos, and web links. You can even paste YouTube video links directly onto the board for reference.

Collaborating in Real-Time

Invite others to collaborate on your board by tapping the Share button. Collaborators can view and edit the board simultaneously, with changes appearing in real-time.

CONVERT HANDWRITING INTO TYPED TEXT

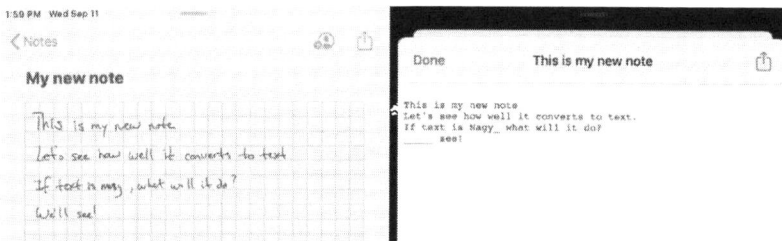

🔧 **Step 1:** Enable Scribble

1. Open the Settings app on your iPad.

2. Scroll down and tap on Apple Pencil.

3. Toggle the Scribble switch to the ON position.

Note: Scribble is enabled by default on supported iPads

📝 **Step 2:** Practice with Scribble

Apple provides a built-in tutorial to familiarize you with Scribble: In Settings > Apple Pencil, tap on Try Scribble.

1. Follow the on-screen instructions to practice writing and see how your handwriting converts to text.

Step 3: Use Scribble in Apps

Scribble works in various apps, including Notes, Pages, Safari, and more. Here's how to use it:

1. Open an app that supports text input (e.g., Notes or Pages).

2. Tap on a text field or area where you can enter text.

3. Use your Apple Pencil to write directly in the text area. Your handwriting will automatically convert to typed text.

Scribble Gestures

Enhance your note-taking with these Scribble gestures:

- Delete a word: Scratch it out with your Apple Pencil.

- Insert text: Touch and hold in a text area until a space opens, then write the new text.

- Join or separate characters: Draw a vertical line between them.

- Select text: Circle the text or draw a line through it to select.

🛠️ Troubleshooting Tips

- Scribble not working? Ensure it's enabled in Settings > Apple Pencil.

- App compatibility: Not all apps support Scribble. Use Apple apps like Notes or Pages for the best experience.

- Handwriting recognition: Write clearly and at a moderate pace to improve accuracy.

MARK UP A SCREENSHOT

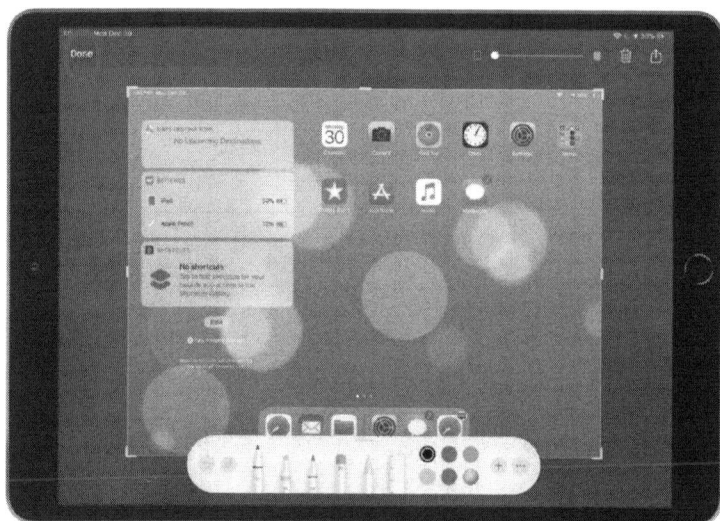

Step 1: Open the Screenshot in Markup

- After taking a screenshot, you'll see a thumbnail appear in the lower-left corner of the screen.

- Tap the thumbnail before it disappears. This opens the screenshot in the Markup editor.

If you took the screenshot using the Apple Pencil swipe gesture, the Markup tools might open automatically.

Step 2: Use Markup Tools with Apple Pencil

At the bottom of the screen, you'll see the Markup toolbar. Here's how to use it:

Draw or Write

- Tap a tool (like the pen, marker, or highlighter).

- Use your Apple Pencil to draw, underline, circle, or write directly on the screenshot.

Change Colour or Thickness

- Tap a colour from the toolbar, or tap the colour wheel for custom colours.

- To adjust line size or opacity:

- Tap the selected tool again (e.g., double-tap the pen icon).
- A menu will pop up with thickness and opacity options.

Erase Mistakes

- Tap the eraser tool to clean up any parts you don't want.
- Some iPads let you double-tap the Apple Pencil to quickly switch to the eraser.

Move Your Markup

- Tap the lasso tool, then draw around the markup you want to move.
- Drag it to a new location on the screen.

Add Extra Elements

Tap the "+" button in the corner to add:

- Text boxes
- Shapes (like arrows, squares, speech bubbles)
- Your signature (if you've saved one)

Step 3: Save or Share Your Marked-Up Screenshot

Once you're happy with your markup:

To Save:

- Tap Done (top left).
- Choose "Save to Photos" or "Save to Files".

To Share:

- Tap the Share icon (a square with an arrow pointing up).
- Choose where to send it—Messages, Mail, Airdrop, or other apps.

To Delete:

- Tap the trash icon if you don't want to keep it.
- Or tap Done → Delete Screenshot.

CHAPTER FIVE:

HOW TO ADD AND EDIT DRAWINGS ON YOUR IPAD USING THE APPLE PENCIL PRO

HOW TO ADD A DRAWING

Getting Started: Setup and Canvas

1 Pair Your Apple Pencil Pro

- Simply **attach it magnetically** to your iPad or pair via Bluetooth – no cables needed!

- Once paired, the Pencil **auto-charges** on the iPad and is ready to use.

2 . Open a Drawing App

- Try built-in apps like **Notes** or **Markup**, or go for creative apps like **Procreate** or **Adobe Fresco**.

- **Create a new canvas**: In Procreate, tap +; in Notes, tap the **pencil icon**.

3 Rest Your Hand and Start Drawing

- Thanks to **palm rejection** and low latency, you can **rest your hand** on the screen and start drawing right away!

Tool Selection and Interface

Most apps have a toolbar with:

- **Brushes** (pens, pencils, markers)

- **Eraser**

- **Colour picker**
- **Shape tools**

👉 In Procreate, for example, you'll see a **colour wheel** and brush options.

- **Tap a brush icon** to choose it.
- **Tap the colour selector** to pick a colour.
- **Hover the Pencil Pro** over icons to preview tools (in supported apps).
- Use **on-screen sliders** to adjust stroke size or opacity.

💡 **Pressure-sensitive strokes**:

- **Press harder** for thick, dark lines.
- **Press lightly** for thin, faint strokes.
- **Tilt** the Pencil to create shading or soft strokes (if supported).

✦ **Quick actions**:

- **Double-tap** the side of Pencil Pro to swap tools (like pen and eraser).
- **Squeeze** the Pencil Pro to access shortcut palettes for undo, redo, colour pick, etc. (if the app supports it).

Using Layers

Layers work like transparent sheets stacked up:

- **Sketch layer**: for rough outlines.

- **Line art layer**: for clean, final lines.

- **Colour and shading layers**: placed **under** the line art layer.

Layers make editing easy—erase or recolour one part without changing the rest.

- Most apps have a **Layers panel** to add or rearrange layers.

Step-by-Step Drawing

Step 1 – Sketch Your Idea

- Start with a **rough sketch**: light shapes and outlines.

- Use basic shapes (circles, ovals, rectangles) to build the figure, then connect with lines.

- Don't stress about perfection—these are just your **guidelines**!

Step 2 – Inking and Outlining

- **Create a new layer above** your sketch.

- Use a clean brush or pen tool to **trace over the sketch** with smooth lines.

- Press harder for thick lines, lighter for details.

- **Erase or hide the sketch layer** when you're happy with your inked lines.

Step 3 – Colouring and Shading

- **Add a new layer below** the ink layer for colours.

- Use the **paint bucket** or **fill tool** (if available), or gently colour in with the brush.

- Pressure and tilt help **control intensity** and create natural shading.

- For **shadows and highlights**, add more layers with slightly darker or lighter colours.

- Use **blending brushes** or the **smudge tool** to create smooth gradients.

Step 4 – Final Touches

- **Zoom in** to refine edges and smooth strokes.

- **Add small details or highlights** to make your drawing pop.

- Use **hover** (if supported) to precisely position small elements before you draw.

HOW TO EDIT DRAWINGS

1. Smooth and Straighten Strokes

☑️ In most drawing apps (like Procreate), you can turn on stabilization features:

- In Procreate, use Streamline or stabilization in brush settings.

- This smooths out wobbly lines automatically.

☑ Light pressure on your Pencil Pro creates thinner, more precise lines.

☑ Try different brushes to see how they respond to pressure and tilt.

2. QuickShape for Perfect Shapes

☑ Draw any shape (line, circle, box), then hold your Pencil at the end of the stroke.

☑ The app will "snap" it into a perfect shape (straight line, circle, rectangle).

☑ Example: Draw a rough box, hold it, and it'll become a sharp, straight-edged box.

Rotate and Snap Shapes

☑ While holding the shape, place a second finger on the screen.

☑ This locks the rotation into fixed angles (like 15° steps in Procreate).

☑ Use this for perfect alignment.

4. Clean Up Stray Marks

☑ Zoom in and use the Eraser tool to delete extra lines or sketch marks.

☑ In Procreate:

- Double-tap your Pencil to toggle eraser/brush.
- Or map the squeeze gesture to switch quickly.
  ☑ Undo mistakes with a two-finger tap — easy and fast!

Tip:
In vector apps like Adobe Fresco, the Vector Trimmer tool automatically deletes intersecting lines to clean up messy sketches. The Paint Inside feature helps fill shapes without spilling outside the lines.

🔶 Erasing Mistakes

☑ Select the Eraser:

- Tap the eraser icon or use Pencil Pro gestures (double-tap or squeeze) to toggle between brush and eraser.

☑ Erase precisely:

- Use a smaller eraser brush for tiny details.
- Tilt your Pencil to control the eraser's angle.
- For large edits, use selection tools (like lasso) to delete specific areas.

☑ Undo and Redo:

- Two-finger tap: Undo.

- Three-finger tap: Redo.

- No worries, you can undo as much as you need!

❖ Recolouring Elements

🍎 Choose Colours

☑ Tap the colour picker (eyedropper) to sample existing colours or adjust new ones in the colour wheel.

☑ In Procreate, drag the colour wheel or hold your Pencil on the canvas to pick a colour.

☑ You can map the squeeze gesture to open the colour palette for quick access.

🍎 Fill Areas

☑ If your outline is closed, drag the colour circle onto it (Procreate's Colour Drop).

☑ In Adobe Fresco, use the Paint Inside tool to fill enclosed shapes cleanly.

🍎 Work in Layers

☑ Add a new layer below your line art for colouring.

☑ This keeps your lines separate and clean.

☑ Rename layers for easy organization.

 Blend and adjust

☑ Use layer blend modes (Multiply, Overlay, etc.) for shading and tints.

☑ Adjust hue, saturation, or brightness of a colour-filled area with colour adjustment tools in your app.

Reshaping and Transforming

☑ Select and Move

- Use the Move/Transform tool (usually a cursor or arrow icon) to select an object or area.

- Drag it to reposition.

☑ **Scale and Rotate**

- Pinch two fingers outward or inward to scale.

- Twist two fingers to rotate.

- Hold one finger for precise 15° rotation steps in Procreate.

☑ Uniform vs. Free Transform

- Uniform: Keeps proportions (square stays square).

- Freeform/Distort: Skews and warps shapes for more creative effects.

- The Barrel Roll feature of the Pencil Pro can rotate brush orientation or even shape orientation in some apps.

Using Layers

Layers help you keep parts of your drawing separate and easy to edit.

☑ Tap the Layers icon (stacked squares) to open the panel.

☑ Tap + to add a new layer.

☑ Touch and hold a layer to drag it up or down in the stack.

☑ Rename layers by tapping the name.

☑ Adjust layer opacity and blending modes for effects like shading and lighting.

☑ In Procreate, you can map the squeeze gesture to "Layer Select" to quickly switch layers.

☀ Adding Effects and Finishing Touches

✅ Adjustments and Filters

- In most apps, go to the Adjustments or Filters menu to apply effects like blur, glow, sharpen, noise, or colour balance.

- In Procreate, use Gaussian Blur or Bloom for soft edges and glow.

✅ Brush Effects

- Try different brushes for unique textures (charcoal, watercolour, etc.).

- Tilt your Pencil for wider strokes or natural shading.

- Adjust pressure for opacity and size changes.

✅ Colour and Lighting

- Add highlights and shadows on separate layers.

- Light pressure for soft shading, harder pressure for bold highlights.

✅ Final Polish

- Zoom out to see your whole artwork.

- Blend edges with a soft eraser or blur brush.

- Double-check layer visibility and order.

- Save or export your artwork!

⟳ Undo and Redo Actions

☑ Undo: Two-finger tap.

☑ Redo: Three-finger tap.

☑ On-screen buttons: Most apps also have Undo/Redo buttons.

☑ Version History: Some apps (like Apple Notes) let you restore earlier versions.

HOW TO SEPARATE A DRAWING INTO PARTS

Apple's productivity apps Pages, Keynote, and Numbers offer a "Select and Scroll" feature that allows you to select, copy, paste, or delete specific parts of your drawings.

1. Enable "Select and Scroll"

- Open your document in Pages, Keynote, or Numbers.

- Tap the More button (three dots) in the toolbar.

- Scroll down and tap Apple Pencil Settings.

- Turn on Select and Scroll.

- If your Apple Pencil Pro supports it, you can enable Double-Tap to Switch, allowing you to toggle "Select and Scroll" on and off by double-tapping the lower part of the Apple Pencil.

2. Select and Copy a Drawing Segment

- Use your Apple Pencil to draw a box around the portion of the drawing you want to separate.

- Double-tap the selected area with your Apple Pencil to copy it.

3. Paste or Delete the Selected Segment

- To paste: Tap in the desired location with your finger to paste the copied section.

- To delete: Once the area is selected, tap the Delete button.

Separating Elements in Procreate

Procreate is a powerful drawing app that allows for detailed control over your artwork through the use of layers.

1. Utilize Layers for Individual Elements

- Open your project in Procreate.

- Tap the Layers panel (two overlapping squares icon).

- Create a new layer for each element you want to separate. This allows you to edit each component independently.

2. Select and Manipulate Specific Elements

- To select content from a layer:

  o Tap the layer once to select it.

- Tap it again to access the Layer Options menu.

- Choose Select to isolate the content.

- To move or transform the selected content:

  - Use the Transform tool (arrow icon) to move, scale, or rotate the selected element.

3. Assign Layer Select to Apple Pencil Pro

- Procreate allows Apple Pencil Pro users to assign Layer Select to the squeeze function:

  - Go to Actions > Prefs > Gesture Controls.

  - Assign Layer Select to the Squeeze gesture.

  - This enables quick selection of layers without touching the screen.

Separating Drawings in the Notes App

The built-in Notes app on iPad offers a straightforward way to separate and manipulate parts of your drawings.

1. Use the Lasso Tool

- Open your note containing the drawing.

- Tap the Markup button (pen icon) to enter drawing mode.

- Select the Lasso tool from the toolbar.

- Draw a loop around the part of the drawing you want to separate.

2. Move, Copy, or Delete the Selected Area

- After selecting the area:

  o To move: Drag the selection to a new location.

  o To copy: Tap and hold the selection, then choose Copy.

  o To delete: Tap and hold the selection, then choose Delete.

🔅 Additional Tips for Apple Pencil Pro Users

- Double-Tap to Switch Tools: If enabled, double-tapping the lower part of the Apple Pencil Pro can switch between the current tool and the eraser or previous tool.

- Preview Tool Effects: Hover the Apple Pencil Pro over the tool palette to preview different tools, colours, and effects before selecting them.

- Tilt for Shading: Tilting the Apple Pencil Pro can produce shading effects, similar to traditional pencils, depending on the app's capabilities.

HOW TO ANIMATE A DRAWING

Getting Started: Setting Up Your Tools, Installing and Updating Animation Apps

- Download and update apps like Procreate, Procreate Dreams, RoughAnimator, FlipaClip, Adobe Fresco, and others (e.g., Animation

Desk, Looom). Updates ensure full support for Pencil Pro.

Enable Stylus Features in Apps

- In each app's settings, turn on stylus input and pressure sensitivity. Example (FlipaClip): Settings → Stage → Enable Stylus Pressure & Stylus Hover Preview. This lets you see a brush tip preview (hover) and control line thickness with pressure.

Configure Apple Pencil Pro Gestures

- In iOS Settings → Apple Pencil, toggle features like double-tap (default: switches brush/eraser), squeeze, and barrel roll. Customize or disable them to fit your workflow.

Apple Pencil Pro Features for Animation

- Pressure Sensitivity: Press harder for thicker strokes or deeper colour (e.g. Procreate brushes respond dynamically).

- Tilt: Tilting shades or blends strokes (many brushes support this by default).

- Hover: View a preview cursor above the canvas before touching down (in FlipaClip: Stylus Hover Preview).

- Double-Tap: Quickly switch tools (e.g., brush/eraser).

- Squeeze: Acts as a shortcut (e.g., in Procreate Dreams, squeeze to play/pause animation).

- Barrel Roll: Rotate the Pencil to adjust brush shape, colour hue, or even transform objects in real time (e.g., Procreate, Dreams).

These tools make drawing more expressive and speed up animation tweaks.

Frame-by-Frame Animation

This classic style means drawing each frame by hand. It's great for the organic movement. Here's how to do it in popular apps:

Procreate (Animation Assist)

1. Enable Animation Assist: Actions (wrench) → Canvas → Animation Assist.

2. Each layer becomes a frame. Groups count as one frame.

3. Onion skinning (ghost images of before/after frames) is on by default.

4. Draw your frame, then tap "+" in the timeline to add the next.

5. Duplicate frames or hold frames to adjust timing.

6. Play ( ) to preview. Use the squeeze to pause or play.

7. Export: Actions → Share → Animated GIF/PNG/MP4.

RoughAnimator

1. Start a new project, set FPS and resolution.

2. Use the Brush/Eraser tools (pressure and tilt supported).

3. Tap "Next Frame" or "+" to create a new blank frame.

4. Toggle Onion Skin with the lightbulb icon.

5. Scrub through frames or hit Play to preview.

6. Export as QuickTime video, GIF, or image sequence.

FlipaClip

1. Create a project and set canvas size & FPS.

2. Draw your first frame (enable pressure & tilt in settings).

3. Tap "+ Frame" to add frames.

4. Enable Onion Skin in the menu.

5. Preview with Play and export as GIF, MP4, or image sequence.

Other Apps (Animation Desk, Looom)

- Similar workflows: create frames, draw, use onion skin, and export.

Keyframe Animation (Motion Twining)

Instead of redrawing every frame, apps like Procreate Dreams and Adobe Fresco automatically tween motion between keyframes.

Procreate Dreams

1. Add artwork to the Timeline (creates a content track).

2. Move the playhead to the start time, tap to add a keyframe (Move & Scale).

3. Move to the end time and reposition the content to set the final keyframe.

4. Dreams fill in the in-between frames.

5. Add keyframes for Warp, Rotation, or Filters.

6. Squeeze to play/pause, barrel roll to adjust keyframe attributes live.

7. Enable Looping in onion skin settings for seamless playback.

Adobe Fresco

- Frame-by-Frame: Select layer → Motion → duplicate/add/delete frames. Use Onion Skin and playback tools.

- Motion Path: Tap Motion → Path to create a path for objects to follow (rotate, fade, grow/shrink, etc.).

Short GIF Loops & Character Animation Tips

- Looping: Match first and last frames (FlipaClip's Looping mode overlays first frames for easy alignment).

- Character Animation: Use separate layers for body parts (head, limbs). Animate each part independently for smooth movement.

- Visual Effects: Add filters and brush effects for extra polish (e.g. barrel-roll to shift colours dynamically).

Exporting Your Animation

- Procreate: Actions → Share → Animated GIF/PNG/MP4. Adjust FPS and loop settings.

- Procreate Dreams: Share as MP4 or image sequence.

- RoughAnimator: Export QuickTime video, GIF, or PNG sequence (great for After Effects).

- FlipaClip: Export MP4, GIF, or frame-by-frame.

- Adobe Fresco: Export MP4 or frame sequences.

💡 Tip: For social media, use GIFs/MP4s. For editing in apps like After Effects, export as PNG sequences.

CHANGE OBJECT TRANSPARENCY IN PAGES ON THE IPAD

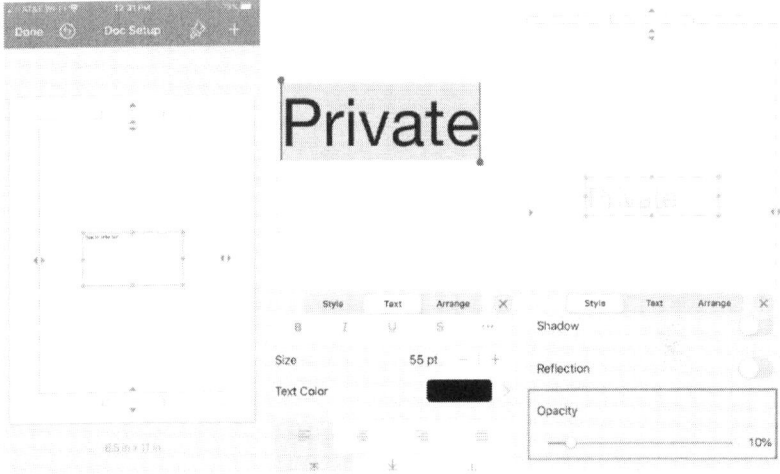

1. Open Your Document and Select the Object

- Launch the Pages app on your iPad.

- Open the document containing the object you wish to adjust.

- Tap on the object to select it. This can be an image, shape, text box, line, arrow, drawing, 3D objects, or video.

2. Access the Format Options

- With the object selected, tap the Format button (paintbrush icon) located at the top of the screen.

3. Adjust the Opacity

- For Drawings:
  - Tap the Drawing tab.
  - Drag the Opacity slider to adjust the transparency level.
  - Alternatively, tap the numerical field next to the slider to enter a specific percentage value (e.g., 50% for half transparency).
- For Other Objects (Images, Shapes, Text Boxes, etc.):
  - Tap the Style tab.
  - Drag the Opacity slider to your desired transparency level.
  - You can also tap the field next to the slider to input an exact percentage.

Adjusting the opacity allows the underlying elements to show through, enabling creative layering effects in your document

CHAPTER SIX:

HOW TO ADD A REFLECTION OR SHADOW IN PAGES ON IPAD.

HOW TO ADD REFLECTION

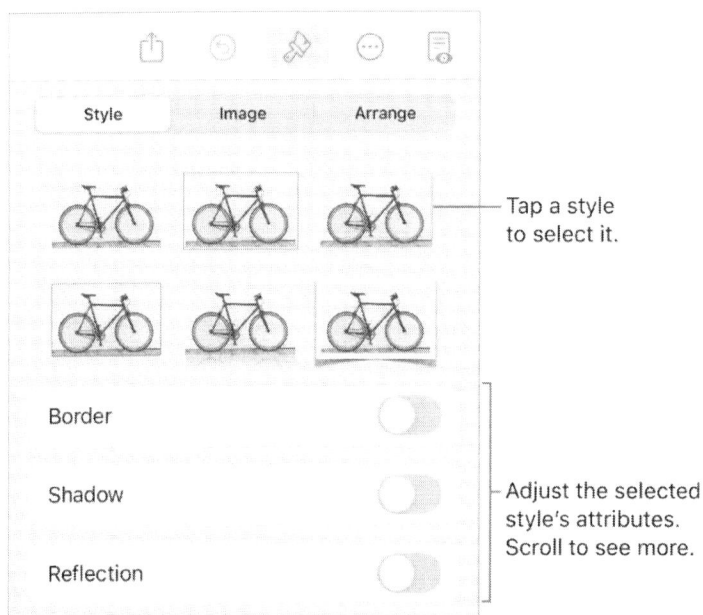

How to Add a Reflection Effect in Pages, Keynote, or Numbers on iPad

 Open the App and Your Document

- Launch Pages, Keynote, or Numbers on your iPad.

- Open the document, presentation, or spreadsheet containing the object you wish to modify.

🍎 Select the Object

- Use your Apple Pencil Pro or finger to tap on the object you want to add a reflection to.

- You can select multiple objects by tapping them individually while holding down a finger on the screen.

🍎 Access the Format Options

- Tap the Format button (paintbrush icon) located at the top of the screen.

- In the Format menu, tap the Style tab.

🍎 Enable and Adjust the Reflection

- Toggle the Reflection option to turn it on.

- A slider will appear; drag it to adjust the intensity of the reflection.

- For precise control, tap the numerical field next to the slider and enter a specific percentage value.

This feature is available for various objects, including images, shapes, text boxes, lines, arrows, and videos.

HOW TO ADD SHADOW

Adding shadows can make your documents, presentations, or drawings look more professional and visually appealing. Let's break it down into two methods:

1) Adding Shadows to Objects in Pages, Keynote, or Numbers

2) Using the Apple Pencil Pro's Virtual Shadow Feature

▇ 1) Adding Shadows in Pages, Keynote, or Numbers

These steps work in any of these apps and can be done using your Apple Pencil for precise selection:

☑ Step 1: Select the Object

- Open your app (Pages, Keynote, or Numbers) and the document you're working on.

- Use your Apple Pencil (or your finger) to tap on the object (image, shape, text box, etc.) you want to add a shadow to.

☑ Step 2: Access Style Settings

- Tap the Format (paintbrush icon) or the ... (more options) button at the top of the screen.

- In the menu that appears, tap Style.

✅ Step 3: Enable Shadow

- Look for the Shadow toggle option and switch it on.

✅ Step 4: Customize the Shadow

- Choose from the shadow styles or adjust the sliders (depending on the app) to change how the shadow looks like its blur, offset, or opacity.

⬛ 2) Using the Apple Pencil Pro's Virtual Shadow Feature

If you have the Apple Pencil Pro, it includes a virtual shadow feature that simulates a shadow as you draw, helping you preview your brush or tool strokes.

✅ Step 1: Make Sure It's Enabled

- Go to Settings > Apple Pencil.
- Ensure the "Shadow" option is turned on.

✅ **Step 2**: Switch Tools and Adjust Shadow

- As you switch tools (like the pen, eraser, or highlighter) within drawing or note-taking apps, the virtual shadow adapts to that tool's shape and size.

- This helps you see how the brush or tool will appear before touching the screen.

✅ **Step 3**: Tilt and Press for Shading Effects

- Tilt your Apple Pencil to see how the virtual shadow changes shape, mimicking a real-life shading effect.

- Press down harder to create darker or thicker shadows, adding depth and texture to your drawing.

WAYS TO USE LAYER, GROUP, AND LOCK OBJECTS IN PAGES ON IPAD

Tap to move the object backwards.

Tap to move the object forward.

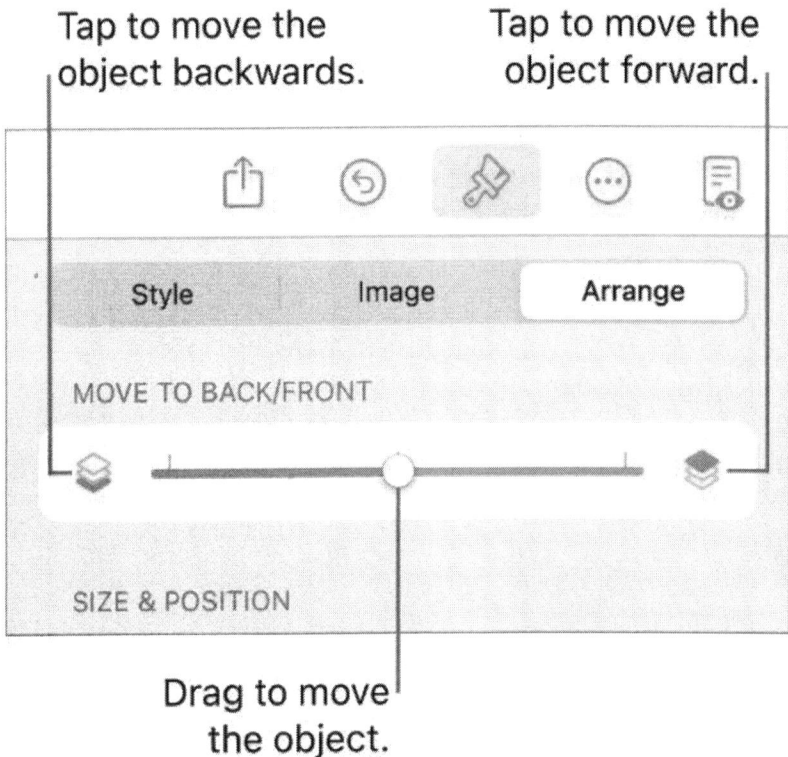

Drag to move the object.

■ Layering Objects

Layering lets you control which objects appear in front of or behind others.

☑ Step 1: Open Your Document

- Launch the Pages app and open the document you want to work on.

☑ Step 2: Overlap Objects

- Drag objects (like images, text boxes, or shapes) so they overlap each other.

☑ Step 3: Arrange Layers

- Tap the object you want to layer.

- Tap the Arrange button (the icon with overlapping squares).

☑ Step 4: Adjust Layer Position

- Use the slider to move the object forward or backward in the stack.

- Alternatively, use the "Bring Forward" or "Send Backward" buttons for quick adjustments.

▨ Grouping Objects

Grouping combines multiple objects into one unit for easier movement and resizing.

☑ Step 1: Select Multiple Objects

- Tap one object, then tap others while holding a finger on the screen to select multiple objects.

☑ Step 2: Access Grouping Options

- Tap the Arrange button.

☑ Step 3: Group the Objects

- Tap the Group button.

- Now you can move or resize the group as if it were a single object!

◼ 3) Locking Objects

Locking objects prevents accidental changes to your layout.

☑ Step 1: Select the Object(s)

- Tap the object or group you want to lock.

☑ Step 2: Open the Arrange Options

- Tap the Arrange button.

☑ Step 3: Lock the Object

- Tap the Lock button.

- The object(s) will now be locked in place and can't be accidentally moved or modified.

HOW TO USE LAYER OBJECT.

🍎 Open the Layers Panel

Most creative apps have a Layers panel or button, typically represented by stacked rectangles or sheets of paper.
Tap this icon to access and manage your layers.

🍎 Create or Select a Layer

- To add a new layer: Tap the "+" or "New Layer" button in the Layers panel.

- To use an existing layer: Simply tap the layer you want to work with.

🍎 Position the Object

- Drag and drop: Move your object onto its new layer using your finger or the Apple Pencil.

- Or, use the Layers panel to move it between different layers.

🍎 Adjust the Stacking Order

- Use the layering controls (like Bring Forward or Send Backward) in the Layers panel to reorder objects.

- This helps you place elements in front of or behind others to achieve the perfect composition.

Lock or Hide Layers

- Lock a layer: Prevent accidental edits by locking it.

- Hide a layer: Temporarily remove it from view while you work on other elements.

HOW TO GROUP OR UNGROUP OBJECTS.

⚠ Note: The exact steps may vary slightly depending on the app you're using (such as Keynote, Pages, or other design tools), but the general process is very similar across most apps.

✅ Grouping Objects

Step 1: Select the Objects

- Tap and hold one object until it's selected.

- Then, tap other objects one by one to select multiple   items.
  (In some apps, you might need to use a multi-select gesture or tap "Select" mode first.)

Step 2: Tap "Group"

- After selecting all the objects, look for a "Group" option.

- This is usually found in the Arrange, Format, or Toolbar menu.

Step 3: Move and Edit as One

- Once grouped, the objects behave like a single unit.

- You can now move, resize, rotate, or apply effects to them all at once.

Ungrouping Objects

Step 1: Select the Grouped Objects

- Tap on the grouped set to select the entire group.

Step 2: Tap "Ungroup."

- Look for the "Ungroup" option, usually in the same place where you found "Group" (Arrange, Format, or Toolbar menu).

Step 3: Work with Individual Elements

- The objects will now be separated.

- You can move, resize, or modify each item individually again.

HOW TO LOCK OR UNLOCK OBJECT

💡 Note: The process may vary slightly depending on the app you're using, but the general steps are similar.

☑ Locking an Object

Step 1: Select the Object

- Open your file or document in the app you're using (e.g., Pages, Keynote).

- Tap on the object (text box, shape, image, etc.) you want to lock.

Step 2: Open the "Arrange" Menu

- Tap the "Arrange" tab or button. In Pages and similar apps, this is usually found in the toolbar at the top or by tapping a three-dot icon (•••).

Step 3: Tap "Lock."

- In the Arrange menu, tap "Lock".

- The object is now fixed in place — it can't be moved, resized, or deleted until it's unlocked.

Unlocking an Object

Step 1: Select the Locked Object

- Tap on the locked object.
  (You may need to tap and hold or double-tap to bring up options.)

Step 2: Tap "Unlock."

- In the same Arrange menu or context menu, tap "Unlock".

- The object is now editable and movable again.

⚒ Extra Notes & Troubleshooting

"Move with Text" Conflict

- If you don't see the "Lock" option, the object may have "Move with Text" enabled.

- To fix this:
  - ○ Select the object
  - ○ Open the Format or Arrange menu
  - ○ Disable "Move with Text."
  - ○ Then try locking again

💼 Using Context Menus or Shortcuts (if supported)

- In some apps, you can tap and hold the object to open a context menu that includes Lock/Unlock.

- If you're using an external keyboard, try:
  - ○ Command (cmd) + Shift + L to lock
  - ○ Command (cmd) + Shift + U to unlock (if supported by the app)

HOW TO POSITION ITEMS

General Positioning with Touch Gestures

These gestures work in most iPad apps that allow object manipulation:

- **Dragging**

  - How: Tap and hold an item, then drag it to a new location using your finger.

  - Best for: Quick repositioning of shapes, text boxes, images, or apps.

- **Swiping (Nudging)**

  - How: In some apps, use two fingers to swipe in a direction to move the item slightly.

  - Best for: Making small, precise adjustments.

- **Rotating**

  - How: Place two fingers on the item and twist gently to rotate it.

  - Best for: Adjusting the angle of shapes, images, or design elements.

- **Resizing**

- How: Tap the object, then drag a corner handle (blue dot for images/shapes, green for text boxes).

- Best for: Scaling objects while maintaining proportions.

- **Nudging with Arrow Controls**

  - How: Some apps (like Pages or Canva) offer arrow buttons for moving items in small steps.

  - Best for: Pixel-perfect alignment and precise placement.

⚒ Precise Positioning in Popular Apps

Here's how to get more control in specific apps:

Pages

- Use the Arrange tab to align objects vertically, horizontally, or distribute them evenly.

- Enable guides for better control over spacing and alignment.

HOW TO MOVE, ROTATE, OR RESIZE AN ITEM

🔄 Moving an Object

Step 1: Select the Object

- Tap the object once to select it.

Step 2: Drag to Reposition

- Tap and hold the selected object.

- Drag it to your desired location on the screen.

✅ *Tip:* Most apps let you move objects freely, but some provide alignment guides or snapping tools to help position items precisely.

↔️ Resizing an Object

Option 1: Use Pinch Gestures

- Select the object.

- Place two fingers on the object and pinch inward to shrink or spread outward to enlarge.

Option 2: Use Resize Handles

- Some apps display blue dots (or green dots for text boxes) around the object when selected.

- Tap and drag a handle to resize in that direction.

🎯 *Tip:* Hold Shift (on external keyboards or certain apps) while dragging to maintain proportions.

🔄 Rotating an Object

Option 1: Two-Finger Rotate Gesture

- Select the object.

- Place two fingers on it and twist them in the direction you want to rotate.

Option 2: Use the Arrange Menu

- In apps like Keynote, Pages, or Canva, tap the object.

- Go to the Arrange tab or format menu.

- Use:

  - A rotation wheel, or

  - Input a degree value for precise angles (e.g., 45° or -90°).

💬 Additional Tips & Tricks

🔒 Screen Rotation (Device Level)

- To rotate your iPad screen, open Control Center by swiping down from the top-right corner.

- Tap the Rotation Lock icon to toggle screen rotation on or off.

  - 🔓 Off = screen rotates freely

  - 🔒 On = screen stays fixed

🛠 App-Specific Tools

- Keynote/Pages/Numbers: Use the *Arrange* panel for precise control.

- Canva: Use *Position*, *Rotate*, and *Resize* from the bottom toolbar.

- myViewBoard and similar apps: Use the Selection Tool to move, scale, and rotate.

CHAPTER SEVEN:

HOW TO PLACE OBJECTS WITH TEXT ON PAGES ON IPAD

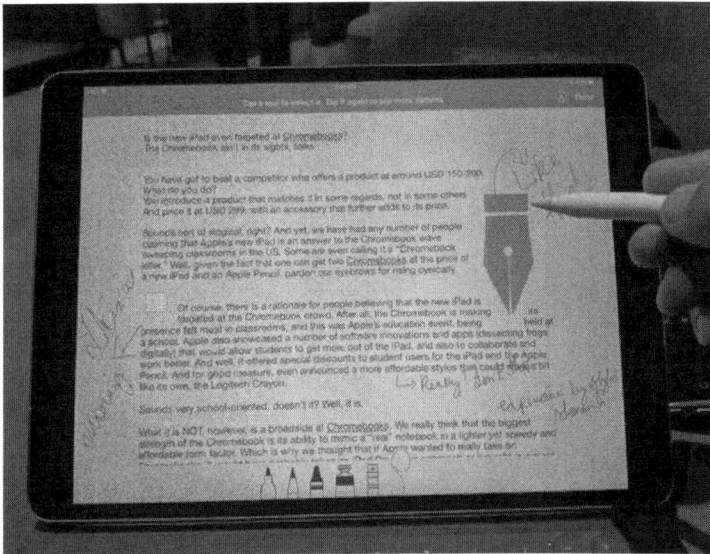

🖊 1 Embedding Objects Within Text

Step 1: Add a Text Box or Shape

- Tap the "+" icon in the toolbar.

- Select **"Text"** or a **shape** to create the space where your object will be embedded.

Step 2: Cut the Object

- Tap the object you want to place within the text.

- Tap **"Cut"** to remove it from its current location.

Step 3: Paste into the Text Box or Shape

- **Double-tap** the text box or shape to place the insertion point where you want the object to appear.

- Tap **"Paste"** to insert the object.

Step 4: Adjust if Needed

- If you see a **clipping indicator** (a small bar at the bottom of the object), **resize the text box or shape** to fully display the object.

2 Placing Objects on the Page and Wrapping Text

Step 1: Add the Object

- Tap the "+" icon to add an object, like an image or shape, to your page.

Step 2: Select the Object

- Tap the object to select it.

Step 3: Choose a Wrap Style

- Tap the **format bar** (the paintbrush icon).

- Tap **"Arrange"**, then tap **"Text Wrap"**.

Step 4: Select a Wrap Option

- Choose how you want the text to flow around the object:

  - **Around the object**

  - **Above and below**

  - **In line with the text**

Step 5: Adjust Spacing

- You can also adjust the **extra space** between the text and the object to fine-tune your layout.

✏ Using Your Apple Pencil

- **Drawing**: Use your Apple Pencil to draw directly on the page or within a shape or text box.

- **Selecting & Scrolling**: Apple Pencil works just like your finger—tap to select objects and swipe to scroll.

- **Annotations**: Apple Pencil makes it easy to mark up your document with handwritten notes and highlights.

HOW TO ANCHOR AN OBJECT TO THE PAGE OR TEXT

🔑 1 Select the Object

Tap on the object you want to anchor, which could be an image, shape, or text box.

⚙ 2 . Access the Arrange Tab

- Tap the Format sidebar icon (usually a paintbrush or similar).

- Then, tap the "Arrange" tab to see the object placement options.

📍 **3 . Choose How to Anchor**

- **Stay on Page:**
  This keeps the object fixed in one spot on the page, no matter how the text or other objects move.

- **Move with Text:**
  This makes the object move along with the text it's anchored to.

  - An anchor point symbol will appear in the text, showing where the object is linked.

  - You can change the anchor point by dragging the object to a new spot in the text.

🖊 4 Adjust Text Wrap (Optional)

If you choose "Move with Text", you can also control how text flows around the object:

- In line with Text

- Around the object

- Above and below

Choose the wrap style that best fits your layout!

HOW TO WRAP TEXT AROUND AN OBJECT

1 . Open Your Document

Open the document in **Pages** on your iPad.

🔍 2 Select the Object

Tap the object you want to wrap text around. This can be an image, shape, or text box.

⚙ 3 . Access the Arrange Tab

- Tap the **Arrange icon** (usually shown as a three-line menu).

- Tap **"Text Wrap"** to see the wrapping options.

📑 4 . Choose a Text Wrap Option

You'll see several options, pick the one that suits your layout:

- **Automatic**: Text flows around the object based on its placement.

- **Around**: Text wraps on all sides of the object.

- **Above and Below**: Text only appears above and below the object.

- **In line with Text**: The object stays on the text's baseline, like a large character.

- **None**: No text wrapping, text won't flow around the object.

🔧 5 Adjust Extra Space (Optional)

Use the **Extra Space slider** to tweak the distance between the object and the text. This helps fine-tune your layout.

✏️ Using Apple Pencil

You can also use your Apple Pencil to draw directly in the document or add hand-drawn shapes. Pages will automatically wrap text around these elements using **Scribble**.

HOW TO SHOW OR HIDE THE RULER ON PAGES ON IPAD

1 Open Your Document

Open the **Pages** app on your iPad and tap to open the document where you want to use the ruler.

2 Show or Hide the Ruler

- Tap the **View Options** button at the top of the screen.

- Tap **"Show Ruler"** to display the ruler.

- If you want to hide the ruler later, tap the **View Options** button again and tap **"Hide Ruler."**

Tips for Using the Ruler

- Use the ruler to adjust **paragraph margins**.

- Set **tab stops** for more precise text alignment.

- Align **text boxes** and **objects** to create clean and professional layouts.

CHAPTER EIGHT:

HOW TO DRAW OR HANDWRITE ON A FREEFORM BOARD ON IPAD

☑ 1 Open Freeform

- Find and **open the Freeform app** on your iPad.

➕ 2 Create or Open a Board

- Tap the "+" **button** to **create a new board**.

- Or, tap on an existing board to **open and edit it.**

✏️ 3 Start Drawing with Apple Pencil

- You can either:

  - Tap the **drawing button** at the top of the screen to activate drawing mode.

  - Or, **start drawing directly** with your Apple Pencil—Freeform will automatically switch to drawing tools!

⚫ 4 Choose Your Drawing Tools

- A **palette of tools** will appear, including:

  - **Pen**

  - **Pencil**

  - **Crayon**

  - **Fill tool**

  - Other creative options!

✏️ 5 Draw, Sketch, or Handwrite

- Use your Apple Pencil to **draw, write, or sketch** directly on the board.

- Let your ideas flow freely!

⚙ 6 Adjust Your Tools

- You can **customize**:
  - ○ **Colour**
  - ○ **Line thickness**
  - ○ **Opacity**
- Tailor your tools to your style and needs.

🎨 7 Fill and Shape Tools

- Use the **Fill tool** to colour in **closed shapes**.
- Use the **Ruler tool** to draw **perfectly straight lines**.

💡 Pro Tip!

The Freeform app and Apple Pencil combo are perfect for **brainstorming, visual note-taking, and collaborating** on ideas with friends or colleagues. 📝 ✨

WAYS TO ADD SHAPES, LINES, ARROWS, AND DIAGRAMS TO A FREEFORM BOARD ON IPAD

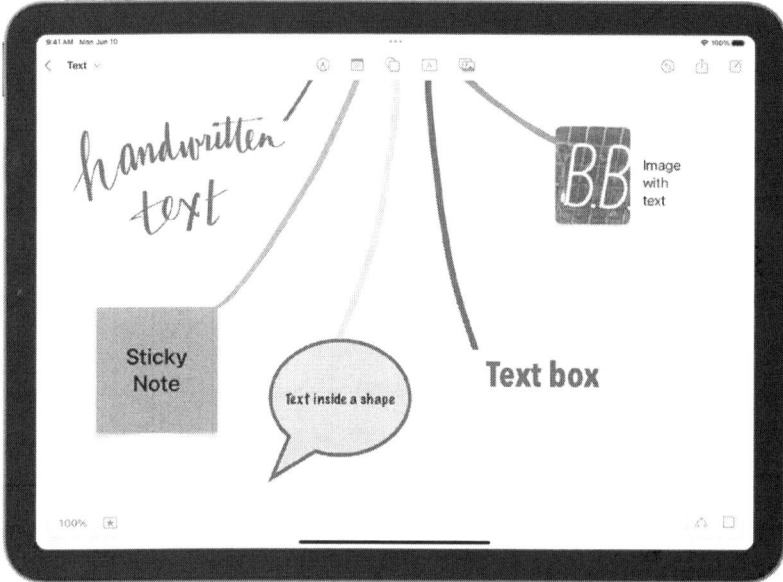

➕ 1 Adding Shapes and Lines

☑ Draw Freehand

- Use your Apple Pencil or finger to sketch shapes and lines directly on the board.

☑ Use the Shape Tool

- Tap the Shape icon at the top of the screen.

- Choose a pre-made shape, line, or arrow from the gallery.

☑ Customize Shapes

- After adding a shape, tap and hold it to access formatting tools.
- You can:
    - Change fill colour
    - Adjust line styles
    - Modify arrow styles

🏹 2 Adding Arrows

☑ Draw Arrows Manually

- Use your Apple Pencil or finger to draw arrows directly on the board.

☑ Use the Arrow Tool

- Tap the Shape icon, then select an arrow from the gallery for quick arrow placement.

🔗 3 Creating Diagrams

☑ Connect Shapes

- Use connectors (lines with arrows) to link shapes and build diagrams.

☑ Align Shapes

- Turn on grid lines and smart guides (if available) to help you align shapes evenly and space them consistently.

✜ 4 Using Editing Tools

☑ Select and Move

- Tap any shape or line to select it, then drag it to your desired location.

☑ Format

- Use the formatting tools to change colours, line styles, and arrow styles.

☑ Resize and Rotate

- Use the handles around the selected shape to resize or rotate it as needed.

✏ 5 Drawing and Smoothing

☑ Free Drawing

- Use the pen or pencil tool to freely draw shapes and lines by hand.

☑ Smooth Lines

- To smooth or straighten your drawn lines, simply tap and hold on the edge of the line.

HOW TO ADD AND FORMAT SHAPES, LINES, AND ARROWS

▤ Freeform

Adding Shapes, Lines, and Arrows:

1. Open the Freeform app and your board.

2. Tap the Add Shape button (a square with a circle) in the toolbar.

3. Select a shape, line, or arrow to add it to the board.

Formatting:

- Tap the shape to select it.

- Use the formatting tools to change fill colour, line style, and endpoints.

Using Apple Pencil:

- Draw shapes directly with Apple Pencil.

- Hold the pencil at the end of the stroke to create a perfect shape.

⚙ 2. Using Freeform

☑ **Open the Freeform app and create a new board.**

☑ **Add items to your diagram:**

- Tap the **plus (+) icon** to add shapes, text, or other elements.

☑ **Connect elements:**

- Use connectors (lines with arrows) to link shapes and create diagrams.

☑ **Freehand drawing:**

- Use the drawing tools (pen, pencil, marker) with your Apple Pencil to add sketches, annotations, or hand-drawn shapes.

HOW TO SPLIT OR COMBINE SHAPE

1. How to Break Apart Shapes

This feature separates a compound shape (a shape made up of multiple pieces) into its parts.

👉 How to do it:

1. Select the compound shape you want to split.

2. Tap the Arrange option in the toolbar.

3. Tap Break Apart.

4. The shape will split into its separate components, which you can move and edit individually.

◆ 2. How to Combine Shapes

🔍 What is it?

Combining shapes lets you create new designs by merging or modifying multiple shapes.

👉 Steps:

1. Select the shapes you want to combine.

2. Tap the Arrange option.

3. Tap Combine Shapes.

4. Choose from these options:

☑ Unite

- Merges the shapes into a single shape.

- Example: Combine a square and a circle to make one unified shape.

☑ Intersect

- Keeps only the overlapping area of the shapes.

- Example: The shared area between a circle and a square becomes the new shape.

☑ Subtract

- Removes the overlapping part of the top shape from the bottom shape.

- Tip: Make sure the shape you want to subtract is on top!

- Example: Subtract a square from a circle to leave a hole.

☑ Exclude

- Creates a new shape by excluding the overlapping area.

- Example: Everything except the overlap stays as part of the new shape.

📝 Example in Action

Imagine you have a circle and a square overlapping:

- **To unite them:**
  Select both shapes → Arrange → Combine Shapes → Unite → They merge into one shape.

- **To subtract the square from the circle:**
  Select the square first (so it's on top) → Select the circle → Arrange → Combine Shapes → Subtract → The square area is removed from the circle.

🖊 Pro Tip: Create Custom Shapes!

Use these features creatively to build unique custom shapes by combining simpler ones, perfect for logos, icons, or infographics.

HOW TO CHANGE SIZE, WIDTH, OR LENGTH

General Steps to Adjust Stroke Size or Width

1. Open the Drawing or Annotation App

- Launch the app you want to use (e.g., Notes, Pages, Procreate, or GoodNotes).

2. Locate the Drawing Toolbar

- Look for a toolbar or a menu with drawing tools; these typically include options like pen, pencil, highlighter, and eraser.

3. Select Your Drawing Tool

- Tap the tool (e.g., pen or pencil) that you want to use. In many apps, tapping the tool again will open more settings.

4. Adjust the Stroke Size or Width

- Once the drawing tool is selected, tap it again or look for a settings icon (gear or sliders).

- Use the slider or presets to change the line thickness, stroke width, or opacity.

5. Use Pressure and Tilt (If supported)

- Apps like Procreate, Adobe Fresco, or Notability support dynamic pen strokes, which means the line thickness changes based on how hard you press or the angle you tilt your Pencil.

- Practice using different pressure levels and angles for a more natural drawing or writing feel.

📌 Important Notes

- App-Specific Controls: Every app has a different interface and features. For example:

  - In Apple Notes, tap the pen tool, then choose from three thickness options.

  - In Procreate, you can finely control brush size and pressure curves.

  - In Pages, tap the drawing tool, then select stroke size and colour.

- Accessibility Settings for Apple Pencil:

  - Go to Settings > Accessibility > Apple Pencil to configure features like double-tap behaviour or squeeze gestures (if available).

- Stroke Length Tip: There's no fixed "stroke length" setting. The length is determined by how far you drag the pencil on the screen. To draw precise lines, use guides or shape tools in supported apps.

QUICK SUMMARY

Feature	Controlled In	How to Adjust
Stroke Width	App toolbar	Tap drawing tool > adjust size
Opacity	App settings	Tap the tool or colour menu
Pressure Sensitivity	Drawing app (if supported)	Varies stroke thickness dynamically
Pencil Gestures	iPad Settings	Settings > Accessibility > Apple Pencil

CHAPTER NINE:

HOW TO USE MARKUP TO ADD TEXT, SHAPES, SIGNATURES, AND MORE TO DOCUMENTS ON IPAD

HOW TO ADD TEXT

🛠 Step-by-Step: Add Text Using Scribble

1. ✅ Enable Scribble

Before using Scribble, make sure it's turned on:

- Go to **Settings > Apple Pencil > Scribble**.
- Toggle **Scribble** ON.

This enables your Apple Pencil to convert handwriting into typed text anywhere you can enter text.

2. ✏️ Add Text in Documents

These are the most common ways to use your Apple Pencil to add text in documents:

📑 In Apps Like Pages or Notes:

- Open your document.

- Tap a **text field** where you want to add text.

- Start writing with your Apple Pencil, and **Scribble will automatically convert your handwriting to typed text**.

- You can erase by scratching out words, or insert text by holding the Pencil where you want to add more.

✏️ In Text Boxes (e.g., Forms or Editable Areas):

- Tap and hold inside the text box until a **Scribble writing space** appears.

- Write your text, and it will instantly convert to type.

📄 Directly in Documents:

- If a text area is editable, you can write directly into it using an Apple Pencil.

- Scribble will recognize the input and format it as typed text.

- Ideal for apps like **Notes**, **Pages**, and **Mail**.

💼 3. Other Options for Adding Text

⌨️ Use Apple Pencil + Keyboard

- You can tap into any text field with your Pencil, then switch to the **on-screen or external keyboard** to type, if preferred.

- Great for hybrid handwriting + typing workflows.

📑 For PDFs and Annotations

- Apps like **Adobe Acrobat**, **GoodNotes**, or **Notability** allow:

  - **Typing into forms**

  - **Adding text annotations**

  - **Handwriting notes directly on PDFs**

166

○ **Highlighting or underlining text**

HOW TO ADD AND EDIT TYPED TEXT

1. Typing with the Onscreen Keyboard

The onscreen keyboard appears automatically when you tap inside any editable text field, such as in the Notes app, Pages, or even in a search bar.

To type using the onscreen keyboard:

- Tap inside a text field to place the cursor.
- The keyboard will appear at the bottom of the screen.
- Begin typing using the displayed keys.

You can also use the predictive text bar above the keyboard to quickly insert suggested words, correct spelling, or complete sentences.

2. Using an External Keyboard

If you prefer the feel of a physical keyboard or want to type more efficiently, you can connect an external Bluetooth or Smart Keyboard to your iPad.

To use an external keyboard:

- Turn on the keyboard and ensure Bluetooth is enabled on your iPad (Settings > Bluetooth).

- Once paired, tap in a text field and start typing, just as you would on a computer.

With a physical keyboard, you can also use common keyboard shortcuts like:

- Command + C to copy

- Command + V to paste

- Command + Z to undo

- Arrow keys to navigate the text

3. Using Scribble with Apple Pencil

Scribble lets you write by hand in any text field, and your iPad will automatically convert it into typed text.

To enable Scribble:

- Go to Settings > Apple Pencil > Scribble and make sure it's turned on.

To use Scribble:

- Simply tap in a text field with your Apple Pencil.

- Begin writing, and your handwriting will be converted into typed text almost instantly.

Scribble also allows you to:

- Scratch out words to delete them
- Circle words to select them
- Draw a vertical line to insert text

4. Typing in Text Boxes (in Certain Apps)

Some apps, such as Notability, GoodNotes, or Pages, allow you to insert text boxes especially useful when combining typed and handwritten notes.

To add a text box:

- Use the app's toolbar to select the text tool.
- Tap or draw where you want the text box to appear.
- Type inside the box using either the onscreen keyboard or an external keyboard.

These boxes can usually be resized or moved around the page, giving you more control over your layout.

5. Editing Text

Once you've entered text, editing it is straightforward:

To edit typed text:

- Select text by tapping and holding a word until the selection handles appear. Drag the handles to adjust the selection range.

- Use the pop-up menu to cut, copy, paste, or replace the selected text.

- Tap once to position the cursor, or double-tap to select a word.

- Use the magnifying glass (tap and hold on the spacebar with two fingers on the onscreen keyboard) to move the cursor precisely.

HOW TO ADD A SHAPE

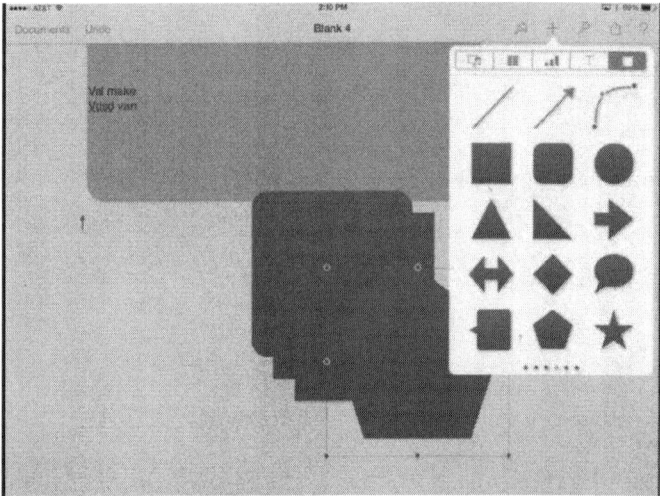

1. Adding Shapes Using Built-In Apple Apps

Pages (Word Processing)

Pages includes a rich shapes library, ideal for documents, flyers, and formatted reports.

To add a shape in Pages:

1. Open a document.
2. Tap the "+" (Add) button at the top of the screen.
3. Select the "Shapes" tab.
4. Browse or search for a specific shape (like arrows, speech bubbles, or charts).
5. Tap the shape to insert it.
6. Customize the shape with colour, outlines, shadows, and even add text inside it.

💡 *Tip: According to Apple Support, you can also add fill colours, change opacity, and layer shapes for more complex designs.*

Keynote (Presentations)

In Keynote, shapes are often used for diagrams and visual emphasis in slides.

To insert a shape in Keynote:

1. Open your presentation.

2. Tap the "+" button.

3. Navigate to the Shapes tab.

4. Select your shape and place it on your slide.

5. Use formatting options to style your shape.

Freeform (Digital Whiteboard)

Freeform allows for a more creative and flexible use of shapes.

To add shapes in Freeform:

1. Open or create a board.

2. Tap the "+" button.

3. Select "Shapes".

4. Choose from a wide variety of preset shapes, lines, and arrows.

🛠 *Bonus: In Freeform, you can combine, subtract, or modify shapes for advanced customization.*

2. Using the Apple Pencil and Markup Tools

The Apple Pencil is a powerful tool for sketching and handwriting, but it's also ideal for drawing perfect shapes using the Markup feature available in many apps.

Supported Apps for Markup Include:

- Notes
- Photos
- Mail
- Files
- Pages (in some document types)

Steps to Draw and Convert Shapes with Apple Pencil:

1. Open a supported app and select a document, image, or note.

2. Tap the Markup icon (typically a pen tip or pencil).

3. Choose a drawing tool such as a pen, marker, or pencil.

4. Draw a shape (e.g., a circle, square, triangle) using your Apple Pencil.

5. Hold the Pencil in place after drawing, and the app will automatically recognize the shape and snap it into a perfect version.

6. You can then resize, move, or change the colour of the shape as needed.

◎ *Pro Tip: In Notes, you can enable "Perfect Shapes" in handwriting settings to automatically refine your sketches.*

3. Drawing and Refining Shapes in Notes and Procreate

Apple Notes

Notes supports both freehand drawing and auto-recognition of standard shapes.

To draw a shape in Notes:

1. Tap the drawing tool (pen icon).

2. Draw a shape freehand using your finger or Apple Pencil.

3. Hold the shape briefly after finishing it to snap it into a clean geometric version.

✦ *This is useful for quick diagrams, sketches, and visual note-taking.*

Procreate (For Artists)

Procreate's QuickShape feature makes it easy to draw clean, perfect shapes.

To use QuickShape in Procreate:

1. Draw a shape freehand.

2. Keep your stylus or finger on the screen at the end of the stroke.

3. The shape will "snap" into a perfect form like a circle, square, or line.

4. To lock proportions (e.g., make a square instead of a rectangle), touch the screen with a second finger while drawing.

✎ *You can use Drawing Assist for more control and symmetry.*

4. Editing and Customizing Shapes

Once your shape is inserted or drawn, most apps provide options to modify it:

- Resize by dragging the shape's corners or edges.

- Rotate using gesture controls or rotation handles.

- Move by tapping and dragging.
- Style with tools to change:
    - Fill colour
    - Outline colour and thickness
    - Drop shadows
    - Gradient fills
    - Text overlays (in apps like Pages or Keynote)

Some apps even allow the layering of multiple shapes or combining them into a complex diagram

HOW TO DRAW A SHAPE

Step 1: Open a Supported App

Start by launching an app that supports shape recognition. Some of the most commonly used include:

- Apple Notes
- Pages
- Freeform
- Mail (when using Markup)

- Photos (for image annotation via Markup)

Each of these apps includes drawing tools that work seamlessly with Apple Pencil.

Step 2: Choose a Drawing Tool

Once you're in the app:

- Tap the Markup icon (often looks like a pen tip).
- Select a drawing tool such as the pen, marker, or pencil.
- You can also pick your preferred line thickness and colour from the toolbar.

Step 3: Draw the Shape

Now, using your Apple Pencil:

- Draw the shape you want (circle, square, star, etc.) in one smooth, continuous stroke.
- Try to keep the outline clear and consistent, don't lift your pencil or break the line.

Step 4: Pause to Transform

After completing the shape:

- Hold your Apple Pencil on the screen for a moment, don't lift it right away.

- The iPad will detect the stroke and automatically convert it into a perfect, geometric version of your shape.

For example:

- A roughly sketched oval becomes a smooth circle.

- A shaky triangle turns into clean, straight lines.

- An irregular arrow becomes precise and symmetrical.

This process is called shape recognition, and it happens almost instantly.

HOW TO ADD YOUR SIGNATURE

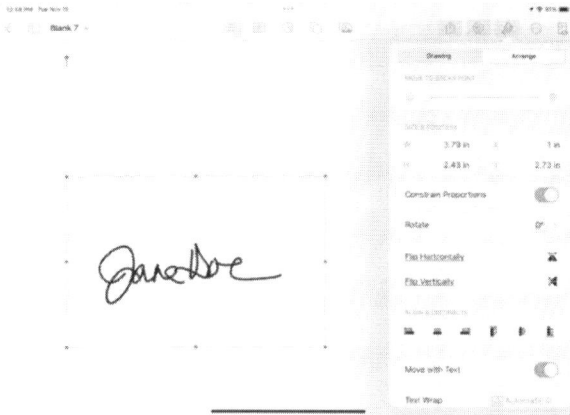

1. Understanding Markup and Signature Tools

Apple's Markup tool is a built-in feature that allows users to draw, highlight, annotate, and sign documents and images. When used with Apple Pencil, it becomes a precise and intuitive way to add a handwritten signature.

You can:

- Create and save your signature.

- Insert it into documents, screenshots, or PDFs.

- Resize and move it as needed.

Once your signature is saved, you can reuse it whenever needed, making future document signing even faster.

2. Step-by-Step: Adding Your Signature

Follow these detailed steps to add your signature using the Markup tools:

Step 1: Open the Markup Toolbar

Start by launching a supported app and opening the file you want to sign. Supported apps include:

- Files (for PDFs and scanned documents)
- Mail (for email attachments)
- Photos (for images or screenshots)
- Notes (for sketches or imported documents)

Once your file is open:

- Tap the Markup button (a pen icon), or
- Tap the arrow next to the Markup button, depending on the app interface.

This opens the Markup toolbar along the bottom or side of the screen.

Step 2: Select "Add Signature"

In the Markup toolbar:

1. Tap the "+" button (usually on the right side).
2. Choose "Add Signature" from the menu that appears.

If you've added a signature before, it will show up here for reuse. Otherwise, continue to create a new one.

Step 3: Create Your Signature

Use your Apple Pencil (or finger, if preferred) to draw your signature in the signature window that appears.

- Sign naturally on the screen.
- If you're not satisfied, tap "Clear" to try again.
- Once you're happy with the result, tap "Done" to save it.

Your signature will now appear in the document and will also be stored for future use.

Step 4: Insert and Adjust the Signature

After tapping "Done":

- Your signature will appear on the page.

- Drag it to the appropriate location (e.g., a signature line).

- Use the blue handles around the signature box to resize it as needed.

- You can also rotate it or delete it by tapping and using the options that appear.

3. Where You Can Use This Feature

The ability to sign documents is available in many native iPad apps:

- Files: Sign PDF forms, scanned documents, and contracts.

- Mail: Open attachments in Markup to sign and return quickly.

- Photos: Add a personal signature to screenshots or images.

- Notes: Sign forms or agreements saved to a note.

This versatility makes it easy to handle paperwork on the go, no printer or scanner required.

HOW TO ADD OR DELETE SIGNATURES AND HOW TO ADD A STICKER WITH MARKUP

Adding a Signature

Here's how to add a new signature using Apple Pencil:

1. **Open the Markup Toolbar**

   o Launch a supported app like Files, Photos, or Notes.

   o Open the document or image you want to sign.

   o Tap the Markup icon (a pen tip) to activate the Markup toolbar.

2. **Tap the "+" Button**

   o In the toolbar, tap the "+" icon (usually in the bottom-right or top-right corner).

3. **Select "Add Signature."**

   o A signature window will appear.

4. **Create Your Signature**

   o Use your Apple Pencil or your finger to draw your signature.

- If you make a mistake, tap "Clear" to start over.

5. Save and Insert

- Once satisfied, tap "Done".

- Your signature will appear on the document.

- Drag it to the desired position and resize it using the corner handles.

Adding a Sticker

Here's how to add a sticker using Markup and your Apple Pencil:

1. **Open a Supported App**
   Open a document or image in an app like **Photos**, **Files**, or **Notes**.

2. **Activate Markup**
   Tap the **Markup icon** to open the toolbar.

3. **Tap the "+" Icon**
   Select **"Stickers"** from the popup menu.

4. **Browse and Select**
   Scroll through the available stickers. Tap one to insert it.

5. **Place and Customize**

- o **Move** the sticker by dragging it.

- o **Resize** it by dragging the corner handles.

- o **Rotate** it using a two-finger twist or by dragging rotation controls (if available).

Stickers can be used to mark important sections, add emphasis, or simply bring a playful tone to your work.

Adjusting Signatures and Stickers

After placing a signature or sticker, you can modify it easily:

- **Move**: Tap and drag to place it precisely where you want.

- **Resize**: Drag the **blue dots** (handles) at the corners.

- **Delete**: Tap once to select, then choose **"Delete"** from the contextual menu.

- **Change Colour or Line Weight** (for signatures): Use the Markup toolbar to choose a new **ink colour** or **thickness**.

Note: These options may vary slightly depending on the app you're using Markup in.

Inserting a Saved Signature

If you've already created a signature, you can insert it again easily:

- Open the Markup toolbar.
- Tap the "+" icon and choose "Add Signature."
- Select your saved signature from the list.
- Tap to insert it into your document, then adjust as needed.

Deleting or Managing Signatures

You can store multiple signatures, but you may wish to update or delete them occasionally. Here's how:

1. Open the Markup toolbar.
2. Tap the "+" icon, then select "Add Signature."
3. In the signature window, tap "Add or Remove Signature" (or "Edit").
4. You'll see a list of your saved signatures. Tap:

- o "Delete" to remove one

- o "+" to add a new one

- o Or tap an existing signature to edit it

These changes will sync across your iCloud-enabled devices.

HOW TO ADD CUSTOM IMAGE DESCRIPTIONS

On the Rocks

A crab ventures out from its safe haven.

Step 1: Open a Supported App

Begin by opening a supported app such as:

- Photos – for pictures and screenshots
- Files – for images or PDFs
- Notes – for images embedded in notes

Then, select the image you want to work with.

Step 2: Launch the Markup Tool

Once the image is open:

1. Tap the Markup button.

   - This icon usually looks like a pen tip and may be found at the bottom or top of the screen.

2. Alternatively, in some apps, you may need to tap the Share button first, then choose Markup from the list of options.

This opens the Markup editing interface, where you can draw, annotate, and now add descriptions.

Step 3: Add a Description

1. In the Markup toolbar, tap the "+" (Add) button.

2. From the pop-up menu, tap "Description."

3. A text box will appear where you can enter your custom description.

Use this space to describe what's in the image clearly and briefly. For example:

- "A child reading a book under a tree."

- "A pie chart showing 2023 revenue by region."

- "A family portrait in front of the Eiffel Tower."

Once finished, tap "Done."

Your custom description is now saved with the image and can be read aloud by VoiceOver.

Tips for Writing Effective Descriptions

- Be concise and clear: Write only what's necessary to understand the image.

- Focus on meaning: Highlight what's most important about the image in context.

- Avoid redundancy: Don't describe elements that are already explained in nearby text.

Image Type	Good Description
Photograph	"Two puppies playing in a grassy park."
Chart	"Line graph showing a steady increase in sales from January to June."
Screenshot	"Home screen with several app icons, including Mail, Safari, and Calendar."

Step 4: Re-Edit or Remove the Description

If you want to change or delete a description:

1. Reopen the image and tap **Markup**.

2. Tap the "+" button again and choose **Description**.

3. Edit the text or delete it entirely, then tap **Done** to save your changes.

HOW TO ENTER TEXT WITH SCRIBBLE ON IPAD

Writing in Any Text Field

- Simply **write with your Apple Pencil directly inside any text field** (such as search bars, message boxes, or form entries).

- Scribble automatically converts your handwriting into typed text as you write.

- Even if your handwriting extends beyond the visible edge of the text box, Scribble will continue converting the text seamlessly.

- A handy **Scribble toolbar** appears while you write, offering useful action shortcuts like **Undo**, **Show Keyboard**, and more, depending on the app you are using.

- You can control this toolbar:
  - Tap the **ellipsis (three dots)** button to access settings.
  - Enable **Auto-minimize** to keep the toolbar out of the way while you write.
  - Tap the minimized toolbar anytime to bring it back.

Using Scribble in Notes and Freeform Apps

- In **Notes** or **Freeform**, you need to turn off the **Markup Switch** to reveal the full tool palette.

- In the palette, select the **Handwriting tool** (the icon immediately left of the pen).

- Now write naturally with your Apple Pencil.

- Scribble converts your handwriting into typed text automatically as you write, making note-taking and brainstorming effortless.

Editing Text with Apple Pencil and Scribble

Scribble doesn't just convert handwriting — it also lets you edit your text fluidly using simple gestures:

- **Delete a Word:** Scratch it out with your Apple Pencil just like crossing out on paper.

- **Insert Text:** Touch and hold anywhere in the text, then write in the space that appears to add new words.

- **Join or Separate Characters:** Draw a vertical line between letters to either merge or split them.

- **Select Text:**
  - Draw a circle around the text you want to select, or underline it.
  - Once selected, editing options like cut, copy, and paste appear.
  - Adjust your selection by dragging the handles at the start or end of the selection.
- **Select a Word:** Double-tap on the word to highlight it quickly.
- **Select a Paragraph:** Triple-tap any word in the paragraph or drag your Apple Pencil over the entire paragraph to select it.

Turning Scribble Off

If you ever want to stop converting your handwriting to typed text, it's easy to disable Scribble:

1. Open the **Settings** app.
2. Go to **Apple Pencil** settings.
3. Toggle **Scribble** off.

Your Apple Pencil will then function without automatically converting handwriting to text.

HOW TO USE APPLE PENCIL TO ENTER TEXT IN NOTES AND FREEFORM

Step 1: Open Notes or Freeform

Start by launching the **Notes** or **Freeform** app on your iPad. Both apps support handwriting input and the Scribble feature for text conversion, but their interfaces differ slightly.

Step 2: Access the Tool Palette

Once inside the app:

- Look for the **ellipsis icon (three dots)** usually located at the top or side of the screen.

- Tap this icon to open the **tool palette**, which contains various writing and drawing tools.

Step 3: Select the Handwriting Tool

Within the tool palette:

- Find the **Handwriting tool**, which typically looks like a pen with a slightly wavy line beside it.

- Tap on this tool to activate handwriting mode.

This switches your Apple Pencil input from free drawing to handwriting recognition.

Step 4: Write with Your Apple Pencil

Now, simply use your Apple Pencil to write directly on the iPad screen. As you write, **Scribble** technology works behind the scenes, recognizing your handwriting and converting it into typed text automatically.

Your handwriting will appear neatly converted in real time, making your notes clean and easy to read or edit later.

Tips for Using Scribble Effectively

- **Write continuously:** Scribble works best when you write in one smooth stroke without lifting your Apple Pencil.

- **Don't worry about perfect handwriting:** Scribble is designed to interpret natural handwriting, so even less-than-perfect penmanship will convert accurately.

- **Use editing gestures:** To delete, insert, or select text, use simple gestures like scratching out words or circling text just as you would on paper.

Why Use Apple Pencil and Scribble in Notes and Freeform?

- **Natural feel:** Writing with the Apple Pencil feels fluid and intuitive, combining the comfort of pen and paper with the power of digital editing.

- **Fast text entry:** You can quickly jot down ideas or text without needing to switch to the keyboard.

- **Improved organization:** Converted typed text is searchable and easy to format, helping you keep your notes organized.

- **Creative flexibility:** Especially in Freeform, you can mix typed text with drawings, diagrams, and images seamlessly.

HOW TO CHOOSE TEXT AND CHANGE IT WITH APPLE PENCIL

1. Open a Note or a Freeform Board

- Launch the **Notes** app to open or create a new note.

- Or, open **Freeform** and tap to start a new board or edit an existing one.

These apps support Apple Pencil input and work seamlessly with Scribble.

2. Access the Handwriting Tool

- In the drawing toolbar (called the **tool palette**), tap the **Handwriting tool**, often represented by a pen icon with a wave.

- This enables Scribble mode, which activates handwriting-to-text conversion.

3. Start Writing with Apple Pencil

- Use your Apple Pencil to write in any blank area or text field.

- Scribble immediately converts your handwriting into typed text.

- You don't need to worry about writing perfectly; Scribble is designed to understand a wide range of handwriting styles.

✦ Scribble Tools: Powerful Gestures for Editing Text

Scribble also allows you to **edit and format text** using simple, intuitive gestures. Here are a few you should know:

- **Delete a word**: Scratch it out with a squiggly line.

- **Insert text**: Touch and hold in a space, then start writing.

- **Join or separate words**: Draw a vertical line between the letters.

- **Select text**: Circle a word or underline it to highlight and edit.

- **Select a word**: Double-tap it with your Apple Pencil.

- **Select a paragraph**: Triple-tap or drag over the paragraph.

These gestures allow for fast, fluid editing, just like working with paper, but smarter.

✦ Bonus Features in Freeform

Freeform isn't just for note-taking; it's a canvas for ideas. Using Apple Pencil in Freeform opens up creative possibilities:

✧ Customizable Handwriting

Even your handwritten notes can be formatted in Freeform:

- Change **font style**, **text size**, and **colour**.
- Make your text stand out or stay subtle, perfect for brainstorming or diagramming.

✧ Adding Objects

- You can insert **text boxes**, **sticky notes**, **photos**, and **shapes**.
- These elements can be moved, resized, or rotated with simple gestures.

✧ Grouping Elements

- Select and **group multiple objects** to move or edit them together.
- This makes organizing your board easy and helps maintain layout consistency.

HOW TO STOP CONVERTING YOUR HANDWRITING TO TEXT

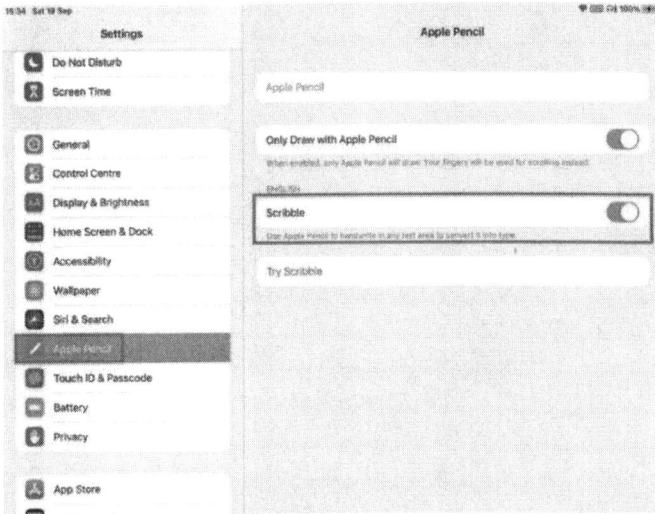

How to Turn Off Scribble

Disabling Scribble is quick and easy. Just follow these steps:

1. Open the Settings App

From your iPad's Home Screen, locate and tap on the Settings icon—it looks like a gray gear.

2. Navigate to Apple Pencil Settings

In the left-hand menu, scroll down until you see Apple Pencil. Tap to open the Apple Pencil preferences.

3. Turn Off Scribble

Under the Apple Pencil settings, look for the option labelled Scribble.

- You'll see a toggle switch next to it.

- Tap the switch to turn Scribble off.

Once toggled off, your iPad will no longer convert handwriting into typed text automatically.

Action	Result
Toggle Scribble ON	Handwriting is converted to typed text.
Toggle Scribble OFF	Apple Pencil acts like a drawing tool only.

HOW TO TAKE AND MARK UP A SCREENSHOT WITH APPLE PENCIL ON IPAD

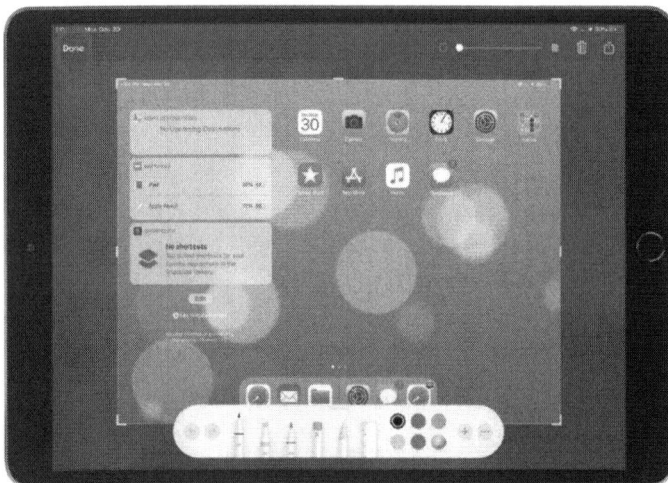

Taking and Annotating a Screenshot with Apple Pencil

1. Capture the Screenshot Instantly

To take a screenshot using your Apple Pencil:

- Swipe upward from the bottom-left corner of your iPad screen using the tip of your Apple Pencil.

- Your screen will briefly flash, and the screenshot will open automatically in the Markup interface, ready for you to edit.

✎. *Tip: If nothing happens, make sure screenshot gestures are enabled in* Settings > Apple Pencil > Left Corner Swipe *and set to* Screenshot.

2. Annotate Using Markup Tools

Once the screenshot appears, the screen becomes your canvas. You'll see a Markup toolbar (usually at the bottom or side of the screen) with an array of tools to choose from.

With your Apple Pencil, you can:

- Write or draw freely.

- Underline, circle, or highlight important areas.

- Use shapes, arrows, or callouts to direct attention.

- Erase, redo, or undo using the dedicated tools.

You can switch between tools like the pen, highlighter, pencil, or eraser by simply tapping their icons in the toolbar.

3. Customize Your Tools

The Markup palette is highly customizable. Tap on any tool to fine-tune its appearance:

- Colour Picker: Choose from preset or custom colours.

- Line Thickness: Adjust the width of your stroke.

- Opacity: Make your markings bold or subtle.

- Add Text: Tap the "+" button to insert typed text.

- Add Shapes: Add boxes, circles, arrows, or custom shapes.

- Insert Signature: Quickly sign a document right on the screenshot.

You can move, resize, or rotate any added text or shape by selecting it and dragging the handles.

4. Save or Share Your Marked-Up Screenshot

Once your annotations are complete:

- Tap Done in the top-left corner.

- Choose whether to:
    - Save to Photos
    - Save to Files
    - Delete Screenshot
    - Share via AirDrop, Messages, Mail, or any app you prefer.

CHAPTER TEN:

TIPS AND TRICKS

HOW TO OPEN THE CONTROL CENTER

Step 1: Use Your Finger to Open Control Center

- Swipe down from the top-right corner of your iPad screen using your finger (not the Apple Pencil).

- This gesture opens the Control Center, where you can access quick settings like Wi-Fi, Bluetooth, brightness, and more.

Tip: The top-right corner is where the battery icon is located.

Step 2: Use Apple Pencil to Interact

- Once the Control Center is open, you can use your Apple Pencil to:
  - Tap on toggles (e.g., Wi-Fi, Bluetooth)
  - Adjust sliders (e.g., brightness, volume)
  - Open additional settings

✖ Step 3: Close Control Center

You can close the Control Center in either of these ways:

- Swipe up from the bottom of the screen with your finger

- Or simply tap anywhere outside the Control Center

📝 Quick Summary

Action	Tool to Use
Open Control Center	Finger (swipe down from top-right)
Interact with controls	Apple Pencil
Close Control Center	Finger (swipe up) or tap the screen

HOW TO OPEN NOTIFICATION CENTER

Opening Notification Center

✅ From the Lock Screen:

- Swipe up from the middle of the screen.

- This will reveal your recent notifications, even before unlocking the iPad.

☑ From the Home Screen or While Using an App:

- Swipe down from the top-center of the screen.

- You can do this from any Home Screen or while using most apps.

☑ From a Full-Screen App (e.g., games or videos):

- Swipe down gently from the very top of the screen.

- You might first see a small tab with an arrow.

- Tap that arrow, then swipe down again to fully open Notification Center.

✖ Interacting with Notifications

Once the Notification Center is open, here's what you can do:

Action	What It Does
Scroll up	View older notifications
Tap a notification	Open the app, it came from
Swipe left on a notification.	Manage, clear, or mute that notification.

| Touch and hold a notification. | See more details or perform quick actions (if supported by the app) |

✖ How to Close Notification Center

You can exit Notification Center in one of these ways:

- **Swipe up from the bottom** of the screen with one finger

- Or, **press the Home button** (on iPads with a physical Home button)

📝 Summary Table

Task	Gesture
Open from Lock Screen	Swipe **up from the middle**
Open from the Home/App screen.	Swipe **down from the top-center**
Open from full-screen app	Swipe down to reveal tab → tap arrow → swipe down again.
Close Notification Center	Swipe up from the bottom or press the Home button.

Interact with notifications	Tap, swipe, or long press.

HOW TO GO TO THE HOME SCREEN

For All iPads (With or Without a Home Button)

Step-by-Step:

1. **Identify the Bottom Edge**

    o Look at the **bottom edge** of your screen (the side closest to where the Home Button would be).

2. **Swipe Up Gesture**

    o Place your finger at the very bottom of the screen.

    o **Swipe straight up** toward the middle or top of the screen.

    o Your current app will close, and you'll be taken to the **Home Screen**.

This gesture works no matter what app you're using or which iPad model you have.

For iPads with a Home Button

If your iPad has a physical Home Button (older models):

- **Tap the Home Button once**
  Instantly returns you to the Home Screen.

- **Double-tap the Home Button**
  Opens the **App Switcher** to view and switch between recently used apps.

HOW TO CREATE QUICK NOTES EVEN WHEN THE IPAD IS LOCKED

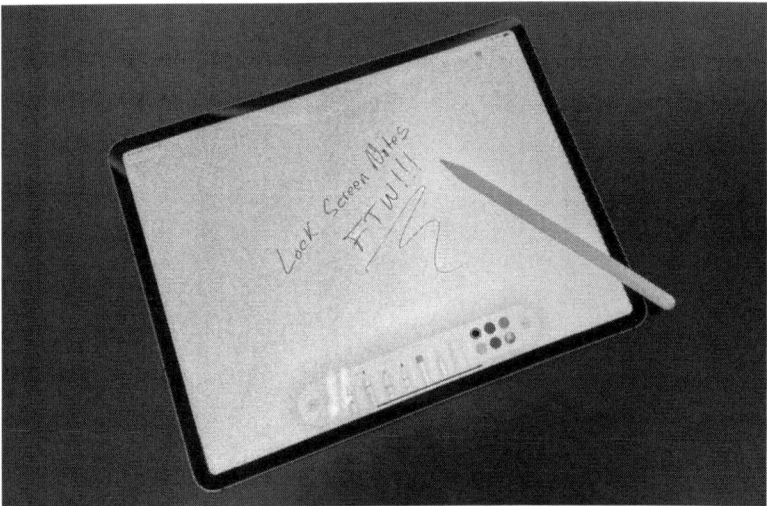

 Method 1: Using Apple Pencil

✔ Step-by-Step:

- Wake your iPad (but don't unlock it).

- Use your Apple Pencil to swipe up from the bottom-right corner of the screen.

- A Quick Note window will appear instantly.

- Start writing or typing your note.

This works even from the Lock Screen, as long as the feature is enabled.

Enable Quick Notes from Lock Screen (If It's Not Working)

1. Open the Settings app.

2. Go to Notes > Access Notes from Lock Screen.

3. Choose one of these options:

    o Always Create a New Note

    o Resume Last Note Created on Lock Screen

    o Resume Last Note Viewed in Notes App

Also:
4. Go to Settings > Apple Pencil and ensure "Left

Corner Swipe" or "Right Corner Swipe" is turned on for Quick Notes.

🖐 Method 2: Using Control Center (Optional)

1. Swipe down from the top-right corner of your iPad to open Control Center.

2. Tap the Quick Note icon (a notepad with a plus symbol).

   o If it's not there:

      ▪ Go to Settings > Control Center

      ▪ Add Quick Note to the list of active controls

⚠ You must unlock the iPad for this method to work.

❌ Can I Type a Quick Note Without an Apple Pencil While Locked?

No. Typing a Quick Note from the Lock Screen is only possible after unlocking the device. The Apple Pencil gesture is the only way to bypass unlocking for notes.

HOW TO BRING UP A SKETCH PAD WINDOW FROM ANYWHERE

Method 1: Using Apple Pencil

Step-by-Step:

1. From any screen (Home Screen, app, or even Lock Screen),

2. Swipe your Apple Pencil from the bottom-right corner of the screen toward the center.

3. A Quick Note window will appear, ready for drawing or handwriting.

4. Start sketching using your Apple Pencil.

💡 You can write, draw, or sketch. Quick Note supports full handwriting input.

🛠 To Enable This Feature (If it's not working):

1. Open Settings.

2. Go to Apple Pencil.

3. Turn on "Right Corner Swipe" (or "Left Corner Swipe" if you prefer).

   ○ This enables Quick Note when you swipe with the Pencil from the screen's corner.

✋ Method 2: Using Control Center (Alternate Way)

If you don't have an Apple Pencil:

1. Swipe down from the top-right corner to open Control Center.

2. Tap the Quick Note icon (a notepad with a plus sign).

3. Use your finger to sketch if your iPad supports it, or type your note.

⚠ Works only when the iPad is unlocked.

HOW TO GRAB A SCREENSHOT USING YOUR APPLE PENCIL (OR FINGER)

✏ **Method 1: Using Apple Pencil**

This is the fastest way to capture and annotate a screenshot.

✔ **Steps:**

1. **Swipe Diagonally**

   ○ Use your Apple Pencil to **swipe up from the bottom-left or bottom-**

right corner of the screen toward the center.

2. **Screenshot Captured**

   ○ Your iPad will take a screenshot immediately.

3. **Markup Tools Appear**

   ○ The screenshot will open in **Markup View**.

   ○ You can **draw, write, highlight, or annotate** using your Apple Pencil.

4. **Share or Save**

   ○ Tap the **Share icon** to send it via AirDrop, Messages, or Mail.

   ○ Or tap **Done** to **save to Photos** or **Files**.

✋ **Method 2: Using Your Finger**

If you don't have an Apple Pencil, you can still use the same corner swipe gesture with your finger (on supported models).

✔ **Steps:**

1. **Swipe from Bottom Corner**

   o Swipe diagonally from the **bottom-left or bottom-right corner** toward the center.

2. **Capture & Annotate**

   o The screenshot is taken, and the Markup tools appear.

   o Use your finger to draw or annotate.

⚠ This gesture may need to be enabled in **Settings > General > Gestures** (if not working).

HOW TO TURN OFF LEFT AND RIGHT CORNER SWIPES TO PREVENT UNNECESSARY ACTIONS

Step 1: Open Accessibility Settings

- Go to **Settings** > **Accessibility** > **Touch**

✅ **Step 2: Enable Touch Accommodations**

- Tap on **Touch Accommodations**

- Toggle the **Touch Accommodations** switch to **ON**

☑ Step 3: Adjust Swipe Gestures

- Tap **Swipe Gestures** (under Touch Accommodations)
- Increase the **"Required Movement"** slider
  - This increases how far you must swipe before the gesture is recognized.
  - Ideal for reducing **accidental swipes**.

☑ Optional: Fine-Tune Additional Touch Settings

- **Hold Duration**
  - Set how long you must touch the screen before it registers a tap.
  - Helps avoid quick, accidental touches.
- **Ignore Repeat**
  - Treats multiple quick taps as a single touch.
  - Useful if you accidentally double-tap.

HOW TO USE SCRIBBLE IN TEXT FIELDS

1. Open a Supported App

- Use apps with text input fields, like:

    - **Notes**

    - **Messages**

    - **Pages**

    - **Safari**

    - **Mail**

2. Tap into a Text Field

- Tap any **text box or input area** with your Apple Pencil.

- A **Scribble toolbar** may appear (floating above the field).

3. Start Writing

- Simply **write with your Apple Pencil** directly into the text field.

- **Scribble will automatically convert** your handwriting into typed text.

🛠️ Scribble Toolbar Features

When it appears, this floating toolbar may include:

Tool	Function
↺ / ↻	Undo/Redo handwriting.
🎤	Enable voice dictation
⌨	Show mini keyboard
↵	Insert a line break
A/A	Adjust text size (in some fields)

HOW TO WRITE WITH APPLE PENCIL AND CONVERT INTO TYPED TEXT

1. Open a Supported App

- Launch **Notes, Freeform**, or any app that supports Scribble (e.g., Word, Safari, or Mail).

2. Access the Tool Palette

- In **Notes or Freeform**: Tap the **"..." (More Options)** button, then tap the **pen tool palette**.

- In **Microsoft Office apps**: Go to the **Draw tab**, then tap the **Scribble Pen icon**.

3. Select the Handwriting Tool

- Tap the **pen icon** from the palette to activate the handwriting tool.

4. Write with Apple Pencil

- Start writing in:
    - **Text fields** (like a search bar or a blank page)
    - **Anywhere editable**
- **Scribble will automatically convert** your handwriting into typed text

✦ Scribble Gestures & Editing Tips

Gesture	Action
Scratch out a word	Deletes it
Touch and hold	Creates space to add text
Draw a vertical line.	Joins or separates characters

Circle word/phrase.	a	Selects it
Double-tap word	a	Selects a word
Triple-tap		Selects a paragraph

Quick Example: Writing in Notes

1. Open **Notes**

2. Tap **"New Note."**

3. Tap the **pen icon**, select a writing tool

4. Use your **Apple Pencil** to write

5. Text is **converted instantly** to typed content

🔍 Bonus: Scribble in Microsoft Word or Excel

1. Open **Microsoft Word**

2. Go to the **Draw tab**

3. Select the **Scribble Pen**

4. Handwrite in a document, and the app converts it to text in real time

HOW TO COPY WHAT YOU'VE ALREADY WRITTEN WITH APPLE PENCIL AS NORMAL TYPED TEXT

Use the built-in "Copy as Text" (Notes, Freeform) or "Ink to Text" (third-party) features:

1. Apple Notes

1. **Open or Create a Note**

   o Write with your Apple Pencil.

2. **Select with the Lasso Tool**

   o Tap the pen icon → choose the lasso (dashed loop).

   o Circle your handwriting.

3. **Copy as Text**

   o In the pop-up menu, tap **Copy as Text**.

   o The converted text is now on your clipboard.

4. **Paste Anywhere**

   o Go to any app, tap the text field, and choose **Paste**.

2. Freeform

1. **Open a Board**

   o Write with your Apple Pencil.

2. **Circle Handwriting**

   o Select the lasso tool, draw around your text.

3. **Copy or Convert**

   o Tap **Copy as Text** (to keep your strokes intact)

   o Or tap **Convert to Text** (replaces handwriting with a text box).

4. **Paste (if "Copy as Text")**

   o Paste the typed text wherever you need it.

3. Third-Party Apps (OneNote, Word for iPad, etc.)

1. **Open Your Document** and switch to the Draw/Ink tab.

2. **Select Handwriting** (usually with a lasso or selection tool).

3. **Tap "Ink to Text"** (or "Convert Handwriting").

4. **Copy/Paste** the converted text into any field or document.

HOW TO TAKE RELEVANT ACTION ON WRITTEN TEXT

1. Selecting Text

The first step is to **select the text** you want to work with. Here are different ways to do it:

✦ Basic Selection (Typed Text)

- **Double-tap**: Selects a single word.

- **Triple-tap**: Selects an entire sentence.

- **Touch and hold + drag**: Selects a paragraph or a larger text block.

✦ Precise Selection (Handwritten Text or Drawings)

- **Lasso Tool (in Markup)**: Use this for precise selection, especially in PDFs or handwritten notes.

- **Apple Pencil**: Circle or underline the text to select it with high precision.

2. Taking Action on Selected Text

Once you've selected the text, here are the main actions you can take:

✦ Editing Options

- Tap the selected text to access options like:
  - **Cut**
  - **Copy**
  - **Paste**
  - **Delete**
  - **Duplicate**

✦ Using Markup

- Open the **Markup toolbar** to:
  - Draw or annotate with Apple Pencil or finger
  - Add shapes, highlights, or handwritten notes

✦ Transcribe Handwriting

- Use handwriting recognition to **convert handwritten text into typed text** (available in Notes or supported apps).

✦ Proofread

- Use built-in features or tools like **Apple Intelligence** to check:
  - Spelling
  - Grammar
  - Word choice
  - Sentence structure

3. Using Apple Intelligence Writing Tools

(Requires iPadOS with Apple Intelligence enabled)

When Apple Intelligence is available, you can take advanced actions like:

✦ Proofread

- Tap the **Apple Intelligence icon** or choose **"Proofread"** from the toolbar to automatically correct errors and suggest improvements.

✦ Rewrite

- Select a sentence or paragraph and choose **"Rewrite"** to rephrase it in a different tone or style.

✦ Summarize

- Highlight a long passage and choose **"Summarize"** to generate a shorter version of the content.

✦ Create Content

- Use prompts to generate new content, such as emails, descriptions, or outlines, based on selected text or ideas.

4. Using Third-Party Apps

Several third-party apps offer even more flexibility and features:

✦ Notability

- Ideal for handwritten notes
- Supports audio recordings, annotations, and PDF imports

✦ Microsoft OneNote

- Great for organized note-taking

- Offers syncing across devices and collaboration tools

✦ Other Options

- **GoodNotes**, **Nebo**, and **PDF Expert** provide rich editing, handwriting-to-text, and annotation capabilities.

5. Using OCR (Optical Character Recognition)

For converting handwritten notes or scanned documents into editable text:

✦ Apps that Support OCR

- **Adobe Scan**
- **Microsoft Lens**
- **Scanbot**
- These apps scan documents and use OCR to turn them into searchable, editable text files.

Example Workflow: Proofreading a Paragraph

1. **Select the paragraph** using touch, Apple Pencil, or the Lasso tool.

2. Tap the **Apple Intelligence icon** (if enabled) or choose **"Proofread"** from the keyboard or context menu.

3. Review suggested edits and accept or reject them as needed.

SIGN PDFS AND DOCUMENTS

Option 1: Using Markup Tools (Preview, Notes, Photos, Files, etc.)

Many built-in apps on the iPad support Markup, including **Notes, Photos, Files, and Mail**. Here's how to sign a document using Markup:

✅ Steps to Sign with Markup

1. **Open the Document**

   - Open the PDF or image-based document in a supported app (like **Files**, **Photos**, or **Notes**).

2. **Access Markup**

   - Tap the **Markup** button (usually a pencil tip icon or "Markup" label).

3. **Add a Signature**

   - In the Markup toolbar, tap the **signature icon** (looks like a cursive pen).

   - Choose **"Add or Remove Signature"**, then tap **"Add Signature."**

4. **Draw Your Signature**

   - Use your **Apple Pencil** (or finger) to sign your name.

5. **Place & Customize Your Signature**

   - Drag the signature to the right spot.

   - Resize or reposition it as needed.

- Tap to adjust **line weight**, **colour**, or **style**.

6. **Save the Document**

   - Tap **"Done"** to apply the signature and save the document.

Option 2: Using Adobe Acrobat Reader (Free App)

If you prefer more features or need to work with complex PDFs, **Adobe Acrobat Reader** is a great alternative.

✅ Steps to Sign in Adobe Acrobat Reader

1. **Open the PDF**

   - Open your document in the **Adobe Acrobat Reader** app.

2. **Open Fill & Sign Mode**

   - Tap the **blue pencil icon** in the bottom right.

   - Select **"Fill & Sign."**

3. **Add a Signature**

   - Tap the **pen icon** at the bottom toolbar.

- Choose **"Add Signature."**

4. **Create Your Signature**

    - Use your **Apple Pencil** to draw your signature.

    - Alternatively, upload a signature using the **camera or image** options.

5. **Save the Signature (Optional)**

    - Toggle **"Save Signature"** to reuse it later.

6. **Insert the Signature**

    - Tap on the area where you want to place your signature.

    - Resize or move it as needed.

7. **Save the PDF**

    - Tap the **share** icon or **"Done"** to export or save the signed PDF.

HOW TO DRAW PERFECT SHAPES

Steps to Draw Perfect Shapes

1. **Open a Supported App**
   Open your document, image, or note in an app

that supports the Markup feature (e.g., Notes or Photos).

2. **Tap the Markup Tool**
Tap the **Markup icon** (usually a pencil tip inside a circle or the word "Markup").

3. **Choose a Drawing Tool**
Select a tool from the Markup toolbar, such as:

   o **Pen**

   o **Marker**

   o **Pencil**

4. **Draw the Shape with Apple Pencil**
Use your Apple Pencil to draw the shape you want. Circle, square, triangle, line, star, etc.

5. **Pause at the End of the Stroke**
After you finish drawing the shape, **hold your Apple Pencil still for a second**.
➤ The iPad will automatically convert your freehand sketch into a **perfectly shaped** version of it.

🔄 **Supported Auto-Corrected Shapes Include:**

- Circles

- Ovals

- Squares and Rectangles

- Triangles

- Stars

- Arrows

- Speech bubbles

- Lines (straight and curved)

HOW TO TILT YOUR APPLE PENCIL TIP

🛠 1. Check Tilt Support in Your App

Tilt functionality is only available in **apps that support it**. Common apps include:

- **Procreate**

- **Apple Notes**

- **Affinity Designer**

- **Adobe Fresco**

- **Concepts**

👉 To enable tilt:.

Open the **brush or tool settings** in your app and look for options like "Tilt," "Angle," or "Tilt Sensitivity."

✏️ 2. How Tilt Works While Drawing

- **Tilt the Apple Pencil** as you draw or write to change the **angle** of contact.

- You'll notice different results depending on:

  - **Tool/brush type** (e.g., pencil vs. marker)

  - **App capabilities**

  - **Brush settings**

📌 Examples:

- **Pencil:** Tilting creates soft, wide shading strokes.

- **Highlighter:** Tilting gives a flatter, broader stroke.

- **Pen/Fountain pen:** May vary in opacity or pressure appearance.

✏️ 3. Experiment with Different Tools

Each brush or pen tool may respond differently to tilt:

- **Soft brushes** may get broader or more transparent when tilted.

- **Marker tools** may simulate flat-edge strokes.

- **Pencil tools** often mimic real pencil shading when held at an angle.

🎨 Open your app's **tool palette** and test how each brush behaves with tilt.

🎛️ 4. Adjust Tilt Sensitivity (If Available)

Some advanced drawing apps let you customize **how tilt affects drawing**:

- **In Procreate:**
  Go to **Brush Studio > Apple Pencil** and adjust:

  - **Tilt Size**

  - **Tilt Opacity**

  - **Tilt Angle**

- **In Adobe Fresco or Affinity apps:** Look for **tilt dynamics** in the brush properties panel.

This lets you fine-tune the effect to match your drawing style.

HOW TO USE PRESSURE SENSITIVITY

✏️ **Part 1: Using Pressure Sensitivity in Drawing & Note-Taking Apps**

✅ **1. Choose a Supported App**

Not all apps support pressure sensitivity. Here are some popular options that do:

- **Procreate**
- **Clip Studio Paint**
- **Adobe Fresco**
- **Affinity Designer**
- **Apple Notes**
- **Notability**

💼 2. Select a Brush or Tool

- Open your chosen app.

- Pick a **brush**, **pen**, or **marker**.

- Most brushes that simulate natural media respond to pressure.

⚙️ 3. Adjust Brush Settings for Pressure Sensitivity

Within the brush settings, look for:

- **Size/Width** – changes line thickness based on pressure

- **Opacity/Flow** – lighter strokes appear more transparent

- **Shape/Jitter/Texture** – advanced apps may vary the texture with pressure

👉 *In Procreate:*
Go to **Brush > Apple Pencil** section to tweak Pressure, Opacity, Size, and more.

🖌️ 4. Experiment with Stroke Pressure

As you draw:

- **Light pressure** = thin, faint lines

- **Heavy pressure** = bold, thick, or opaque strokes

This allows for dynamic control of line art, shading, calligraphy, and detailed notes.

⚙ Part 2: Adjusting Apple Pencil Pressure Settings in iPad Settings

Note: Some advanced pressure settings (like pressure curves) may only appear with **Apple Pencil Pro** or in supported apps like Procreate.

⚙ 1. Open iPad Settings

Go to **Settings > Accessibility > Apple Pencil**.

🔧 2. Adjust Hardware Controls

Depending on your iPad and Apple Pencil model:

- **Squeeze Gesture** (Apple Pencil Pro): Customize what happens when you squeeze.

- **Double Tap Gesture** (Apple Pencil 2nd Gen and Pro): Assign actions like switching tools, erasing, or opening the colour picker.

✏ 3. Pressure & Smoothing (if available)

If your iPad supports it:

- Tap **"Pressure & Smoothing"**
- Adjust the **pressure curve** to control how sensitive the Pencil is to your touch.
  - ○ Steeper curve = faster changes in stroke
  - ○ Flatter curve = more subtle control
- Adjust **smoothing** for more natural lines

🛠 Troubleshooting Pressure Sensitivity Issues

DOUBLE-TAP TO SWITCH BETWEEN THE TOOLS

⚙ How to Enable and Customize Double-Tap

❄ Step-by-Step Instructions:

1. **Open Settings**
   Go to the **Settings app** on your iPad.

2. **Tap on "Apple Pencil."**
   You'll see options for your Apple Pencil features.

3. **Find the "Double Tap" Section**
   This controls what happens when you double-tap the flat side of your Pencil.

4. **Choose an Action**
   You'll see several options:

   - **Switch between the current tool and eraser** (great for drawing/notes)

   - **Switch between the current tool and the last used tool**

   - **Show colour palette**

   - **Off** (disables double-tap)

🔄 How to Use It While Drawing or Writing

Once configured:

- **Double-tap** the flat side of the Pencil near the tip

- It will instantly perform your selected action

  - Switch tools

- Show palette
- Toggle eraser, etc.

💡 *Example:* In **Procreate**, you can double-tap to quickly switch between your brush and the eraser, ideal for fast sketching.

HOW TO DRAW ON A PIECE OF ACTUAL PAPER WITH YOUR APPLE PENCIL AND HAVE IT APPEAR ON YOUR IPAD

By default, the **Apple Pencil only works directly on the iPad screen**, not on physical paper. However, you can simulate drawing on paper using a **paper overlay** or **special third-party tools**. Here's how to do it effectively:

✅ Method 1: Use a Paper Overlay on the iPad Screen

✨ What You'll Need:

- **Apple Pencil Pro**
- **iPad**

- **Paperlike or similar matte screen protector**
- **A thin piece of real paper**
- **Drawing app (like Procreate, Notes, etc.)**

🔧 How It Works:

This method gives the illusion of drawing on paper by placing a real sheet of paper over your iPad:

📌 Steps:

1. **Apply a matte screen protector**
   Use one like **Paperlike** to improve your Pencil grip and prevent slippage when writing over paper.

2. **Open your drawing app.**
   Launch any compatible app (e.g., Apple Notes, Procreate, Adobe Fresco).

3. **Lay a thin sheet of paper on top of the iPad.**
   Use plain printer paper; too thick and the Pencil might not register.

4. **Start drawing with the Apple Pencil.**
   The iPad will still detect Pencil input through

the paper. Your drawing appears on the screen as you draw on the paper surface.

5. **Secure the paper if needed.**
   Use washi tape or a magnetic case to lightly hold the paper in place.

⚠ *Note: This doesn't scan or digitize marks made with traditional pens or pencils. It only works because Apple Pencil's signal goes through thin paper.*

☑ Method 2: Use Third-Party Smart Pads (for Actual Ink on Paper)

If you want to **draw with ink on paper** and have it appear digitally on your iPad, you'll need a **smart pad** or **digital writing tablet** like:

◆ 1. Wacom Bamboo Slate or Folio

- Write or draw on **real paper** using a **smart pen**.

- The pen and pad track your strokes and sync them to your iPad using the **Wacom Inkspace app**.

◆ 2. Remarkable Tablet (with Connect)

- While not Apple Pencil-based, it's a dedicated writing tablet that syncs with iPad or iPhone via cloud and app integration.

◆ 3. Moleskine Smart Writing Set

- Includes a smart notebook and pen that transmits strokes to an app in real time.

● *Apple Pencil **cannot draw on traditional paper** and send it to the iPad without touching the screen. These tools are the only workaround if you need real pen-to-paper syncing.*

◎ Summary: Best Options

Method	Tools Needed	Result
Paper overlay on iPad	Thin paper + Apple Pencil + drawing app	Real paper feels with live digital strokes

Smartpad with ink & sync	Wacom Slate / Moleskine / reMarkable	Actual ink captured and synced to iPad
Apple Pencil only (no paper)	iPad + app	Most precise, fully digital drawing

HOW TO DRAW IN EMAILS

🖋 Part 1: Draw on Email Attachments

✅ Supported File Types:

- PDF
- Images (JPEG, PNG)
- Videos (some apps allow frame-by-frame markup)

❄ Steps:

1. **Open the Mail App**

   o Launch the **Mail** app on your iPad.

2. **Open the Email with the Attachment**

   o Tap to open the email that contains the file you want to annotate.

3. **Tap the Attachment**

   o Open the PDF or image you want to draw on.

4. **Tap the Markup Icon**

   o Look for the **Markup** icon (a pen tip inside a circle or a toolbox symbol).

   o This opens the **drawing and annotation tools**.

5. **Use Your Apple Pencil Pro to Annotate**

   o Draw, write, or highlight using tools like:

      ▪ Pen

      ▪ Pencil

      ▪ Marker

      ▪ Eraser

      ▪ Shapes and colours

- Use **Apple Pencil Pro's squeeze gesture** to open the tool palette or switch tools (customizable in Settings).

6. **Save or Send**

- Tap **"Done"** when finished.

- Choose to **reply with the annotated file**, **create a new message**, or **save** the changes to Files or Photos.

Part 2: Insert a Drawing into a New Email

Steps:

1. **Open the Mail App and Compose a New Message**

- Tap the **compose icon** to start a new email.

2. **Access the Drawing Tool**

- In the body of the email, **tap and hold**, then choose **"Insert Drawing"** (you may see a pencil or sketch icon depending on your iOS version).

3. **Create Your Drawing**

- Use your **Apple Pencil Pro** to draw using the available tools.

- Customize with colour, brush size, and tool palette.

4. **Insert the Drawing**

- Tap **"Done,"** and the drawing will be automatically inserted into the body of your email.

🔍 **Advanced Apple Pencil Pro Features in Mail**

Feature	Description
Squeeze Gesture	Customize to open tools or switch between the brush/eraser.
Hover Preview	Hover over the canvas to preview strokes before you draw.
Haptic Feedback	Get tactile responses when switching tools or completing gestures.
Scribble	Handwrite in any text field and it converts to typed text instantly.
Double-Tap Gesture	Set to switch tools, show colour palette, or undo/redo (adjustable in Settings).

HOW TO USE TWO FINGERS TO SCROLL WHEN DRAWING WITH APPLE PENCIL

✳ **Basic Scrolling Techniques While Drawing**

✅ **1. Scroll with One Finger While Using Apple Pencil**

- When the **Apple Pencil is in use**, use **one finger** to scroll.

- This is helpful in drawing apps like **Procreate, Notes, or GoodNotes** where pencil input is for drawing and finger input is for navigation.

✋ *Use your finger to pan or zoom, while your Pencil remains dedicated to drawing.*

✅ **2. Scroll with Two Fingers When Not Using Apple Pencil**

- If you're only using your **finger**, use **two fingers** to scroll.

- This helps prevent accidental marks on the canvas if touch input is also being used for drawing.

✅ 3. Disable Drawing with Finger in Certain Apps

In apps like **Pages, Numbers, and Keynote**, you can **turn off finger drawing**, allowing you to:

- Draw with Apple Pencil
- Scroll and interact with your finger without leaving marks

📌 Steps:

1. Open the app (e.g., Pages)
2. Tap the **More** (•••) menu or settings icon
3. Toggle **"Draw with Finger"** to **Off**

💡 *This gives you a better experience by separating touch input from Pencil input.*

✐ Apple Pencil Pro Features for Input Control

✦ 4. Double-Tap to Switch Tools

- On Apple Pencil (2nd Gen or Pro), **double-tap the flat side** to switch between:
  - ○ Current tool and eraser
  - ○ Current tool and last used tool
  - ○ Show colour palette (customizable)

✦ Customize in Settings:

- Go to **Settings > Apple Pencil > Double-Tap**
- Choose your preferred action

⊟ *This allows for quick tool switching without touching the screen UI.*

⚙ Tips for Better Navigation While Drawing

Tip	Description
Use Canvas Resize/Move	Apps like Procreate let you use two-finger gestures to zoom, rotate, and scroll.

Enable Palm Rejection	Automatically active with Apple Pencil prevents your hand from causing marks.
Use Sidebar Tools	Many drawing apps include scroll/zoom modes or gesture toggles on the screen.

HOW TO TURN HOVER OFF OR ON

🔤 1. Turn Hover Typing on or Off

Hover Typing enlarges the text field you're typing into, making it easier to see, ideal for users with low vision or who prefer an enhanced preview.

📌 Steps to Enable/Disable Hover Typing:

1. Open the **Settings** app on your iPad.

2. Tap **Accessibility**.

3. Scroll down and select **Hover Text**.

4. Tap on **Hover Typing**.

5. Toggle the switch to turn **Hover Typing on** or **off**.

💡 *When turned on, a magnified text window appears near the typing area, which can be repositioned.*

🖊 2. Turn Apple Pencil Hover on or Off

Apple Pencil Hover shows a visual preview of the stroke, shape, or brush before it touches the screen. It's supported on M2 iPad Pro models and works best with Apple Pencil (2nd Gen or Pro).

✦ Steps to Enable/Disable Apple Pencil Hover:

1. Open the **Settings** app on your iPad.

2. Tap **Apple Pencil**.

3. Find the **Hover** option.

4. Toggle the switch to turn it **on** or **off**.

When enabled, hovering the Apple Pencil (1–12 mm above the screen) shows preview effects in supported apps like Procreate, Notes, and Safari.

🔧 Additional Notes & Troubleshooting

☑ Why Use Hover Typing?

- Helps users who need visual support while typing.

- Enlarges text boxes and cursor location for better accuracy.

✅ Why Use Apple Pencil Hover?

- Enhances precision by showing a preview before drawing.

- Useful for detailed work like digital art and note annotation.

Printed in Dunstable, United Kingdom